# Contents

## SECTION D: CASE STUDIES

# Acknowledgements

The author and publishers are grateful to the following for permission to reproduce material: Welsh Joint Education Committee, Times Newspapers Limited, Ewan Macnaughton Associates for The Telegraph PLC, The Financial Times Limited, Newspaper Publishing PLC for The Independent, The Observer, The Western Mail and Lloyds Bank plc. Every effort has been made to contact copyright holders, and we apologise if any have been overlooked.

The author would also like to thank her family and her students at Bishop Hedley High School for their support and encouragement during the preparation of this book.

# Using this book

## Introduction

There are four separate sections to this book and teachers and students are invited to dip into these sections at a time and frequency which is best suited to their individual requirements and those of their 'A' level examination board. The degree of difficulty and the skills required by the student increase not only from one section to another, but within each section. In other words, this book provides off-the-shelf, differentiated assignments.

Perhaps the greatest attraction of this book, however, is that it not only provides the data and the questions, but also the answers. These answers are provided by the author as possible solutions to the set questions, but as chief examiners are anxious to point out, students may arrive at different, but equally valid answers. Teachers and students alike should bear this in mind! The answers, then, are one economist's viewpoint but, even so, they will provide a good anchor point for assessment by the teacher or for self-assessment by the student.

## Section outlines

### Section A

The questions here are focused data response questions and answers. The data are partly hypothetical and partly 'live'. The questions can be used to reinforce classwork or for homework. They are most suited to those students starting out in economics and the helpful hints which accompany the data supply a little bit of a kick-start.

### Section B

In this section, the data are lengthier and 'live'. The questions are still reasonably focused but there is a tendency to widen the scope a little more. Skills and techniques become rather more demanding. Again the questions can be used for either classroom reinforcement or for homework. The first ten data assignments (numbers 11 to 20) are supplied with helpful hints but the remaining questions in this section are free response.

### Section C

The ten data assignments in this section (numbers 26 to 35) are based on live data and they require the higher level skills of evaluation, analysis and application in greater proportion than the questions in the earlier sections. Each data assignment is accompanied by a student guide which will help

# Success in Data Response
# for A Level Economics

# Success in Data Response for A Level Economics

Glenys Jones

Stanley Thornes Publishers Ltd

First published in 1996 by
Stanley Thornes Publishers Ltd
Ellenborough House
Wellington Street
Cheltenham
GL50 1YW
UK

96 97 98 99 00 / 10 9 8 7 6 5 4 3 2 1

A catalogue record for this book is available from The British Library.

ISBN 0 7487 2787 6

Typeset by Florencetype Ltd, Stoodleigh, Devon
Printed and bound in Great Britain by
Scotprint Ltd, Musselburgh

students get started. Obviously, teachers may want to use these questions to assess in formal examination conditions and so the student guide may be omitted if required. Each question crosses topic boundaries which helps students to understand that economics cannot be conveniently compartmentalised.

## Section D

Some examination boards now offer case studies as part of their examination series. The assignments in this section provide practice of this type of case study-based question. The data are varied and higher level skills, again, are required. These case studies might prove useful for the mock-examinations.

## Note

For the convenience of teachers and students there is a table at the back of this book which indicates the topic content of each set of questions.

Before students attempt questions from any section it is advisable for them to read carefully the following *Guide to answering data response questions*. This provides general guidance on how to approach data response questions.

# A guide to answering data response questions

1 Don't panic – there must be something you can do.
2 The best answers mix economic theory with extracted data.
3 Never copy chunks straight from the data – the very least you can do is interpret the information in your own words.
4 Check the mark weighting for each part of the question. This will give a relative guide to the importance of each question part. Data response questions can gain full allocated marks with a short paragraph answer; they are not intended to be full length.
5 Take a careful look at titles and headings. These are sometimes clues to the subject content which follows. Look in particular at headings to numerical data – there is a vast difference between percentage change and absolute numerical values.
6 Anything written in italics (or emphasised in other ways) in questions needs a careful examination and interpretation. The examiner is asking you to focus on this in particular.
7 Do *not* try to absorb vast amounts of numerical data in one go. Look for trends rather than absolute levels.
8 Go through each data paragraph carefully and jot down the main points, especially if you can read the 'economic theory' between the lines. Do not try to rephrase the whole of the paragraph – a short note to jog your memory is sufficient.
9 Look for 'command' words in each of the questions and respond accordingly. For example:

| Word | What it means |
| --- | --- |
| Explain | To make clear. To give details of. |
| Describe | To give the features or characteristics of. |
| | To represent the qualities of. |
| Analyse | To examine critically part by part. |
| | To get to the bottom of something step by step. |
| Compare/ contrast | To point out the likenesses and differences. |
| Evaluate | To appraise or determine the value of. |
| | To state the worth of. |
| Consider | To examine carefully. To arrive at an opinion of. |
| Discuss | To debate. To consider for and against. |

# SECTION A: GETTING STARTED

# Rightway Electronics PLC

Rightway Electronics PLC manufactures printed circuit boards (PCBs). It currently has a fixed quantity of <u>capital equipment</u>, but is able to vary the quantity of workers and materials it uses in the production of PCBs. The following table gives information regarding resource input and PCB output for the firm (in units):

**capital equipment**
machinery and tools

| Capital equipment | Materials/ workers | Total production |
|---|---|---|
| 50 | 1 | 50 |
| 50 | 2 | 100 |
| 50 | 3 | 210 |
| 50 | 4 | 330 |
| 50 | 5 | 400 |
| 50 | 6 | 470 |
| 50 | 7 | 530 |
| 50 | 8 | 520 |
| 50 | 9 | 500 |
| 50 | 10 | 480 |

**total production**
the number of PCBs produced

In the long term, Rightway Electronics can totally alter its <u>scale</u> of production by altering all of its factors of production – including capital equipment. However, Rightway must be aware that increasing its scale of production can, eventually, result in <u>diseconomies of scale.</u>

**scale**
the actual size of the firm

**diseconomies of scale**
problems caused by over-expansion, causing average production costs to rise

## Questions

a  In the short term, at what combination of resources does *diminishing returns* set in? **(5)**

b  What causes such diminishing returns and what is the implication for <u>marginal production costs</u>? **(8)**

c  In the long term, the firm might benefit from <u>economies of scale</u> through expansion. What sort of economies might be applicable to this firm? **(7)**

d  What typical diseconomies could face Rightway Electronics if it continues to increase its scale of production? **(5)**

**marginal production costs**
the extra production costs caused by producing more PCBs

**economies of scale**
the savings or benefits from expansion allowing average production costs to fall

# West Midshire Trust Hospital

The West Midshire is a NHS trust hospital and has an <u>annual budget</u> of £40 million. This budget has to provide for the full range of hospital services – from staff wages to equipment and medicines. The current waiting time for a hip replacement operation is six months and the waiting time for a cataract removal is five months. The Manager of the West Midshire, Tom Pritchard, expresses his regret at these waiting times for what are medically regarded as quite simple operations. However, he stresses that the limited <u>resources</u> of the hospital has meant that choices in the provision of various services has had to be taken by the hospital management team. He further commented that the hospital, in making these choices, was responding to the demands of its clients – the <u>fund holding GPs</u> in the area.

**annual budget**
available finance

**resources**
staff, drugs, operating time, equipment

**fund holding GPs**
GPs who are given their funds directly from government to spend as they see fit

## Questions

**a** Why is health care, like education, mainly provided by the state? **(5)**

**b** Using your knowledge of demand and supply analysis, explain why waiting lists are a feature of the NHS system. **(10)**

**c** Using the data above, explain the concept of *opportunity cost* as applied to the health service. **(5)**

**d** How has the government attempted to increase efficiency and competition within the NHS? **(5)**

# Assembly Techniques Limited

Assembly Techniques is a small company which specialises in the assembly of printed circuit boards (PCBs). Its productive capacity, given its fixed machinery and premises, is 1500 boards per week. The company currently produces 1000 boards and estimates its costs to be as follows:

Total fixed costs = £2,000 per week

Average variable costs = £4 per PCB

The average weekly revenue from selling the 1000 boards is £9000.

Under the present lease terms the weekly rent on the factory is to be increased from £250 to £500 and the Marketing Director has recently estimated that if the company reduces the price of the completed PCBs by 10% sales would expand by 20%.

## Questions

a  How much weekly profit is currently made by Assembly
   Techniques?                                                  (5)
b  Calculate the price elasticity of demand for the PCBs as estimated
   by the Marketing Director. What factors tend to affect the price
   elasticity of demand for goods and services?                (10)
c  What do you think the firm should do in terms of its price and
   output policy in response to the future rent increase on the factory?
   Explain any assumptions you make.                           (10)

**Note:** the elasticity coefficent is given by:

$$\frac{\text{Percentage change in quantity demanded}}{\text{Percentage change in price}}$$

**productive capacity**
maximum production
**fixed machinery and premises**
short-term fixed factors and fixed costs
**total fixed costs**
these (e.g. rent) stay the same regardless of output
**average variable costs**
these (e.g. materials) vary with production

**price elasticity of demand**
a measure of how demand changes in response to price changes

**Data 4**

# Production possibilities: Utopia

The <u>production possibility curve</u> for consumer and producer goods for Utopia is shown below.

**production possibility curve**
a 2D diagram showing maximum potential production of two goods or services

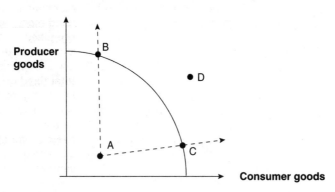

*Production possibility curve*

Currently, Utopia produces a combination of consumer and <u>producer goods</u> – this is A on the diagram. The Utopian government is concerned about current production and aims for the economy to move to a combination of goods as represented by a point on the production possibility curve itself – either B or C.

**producer goods**
investment goods (e.g. machines, equipment, tools)

## Questions

**a** What basic economic principles are illustrated by the concept of a 'production possibility curve'? **(10)**

**b** What do you think concerns the Utopian government about current production as represented by A? **(5)**

**c** If the Utopian government is interested in long-term rather than short-term growth, which growth path do you think it should be pursuing – AB or AC? Explain your answer. **(5)**

**d** Examine the combination of goods as represented by point D. Although Utopia cannot currently produce this combination, it may be able to do so in future. Explain how this might arise. **(5)**

# Star Enterprise

Star Enterprise is a producer of records, tapes and CDs. It has <u>exclusive</u> recording contracts with many famous bands and singers. One such band is Blot which has recently had a number 1 in the charts for five consecutive weeks.

The diagram below illustrates the likely demand for the CD version of Blot's next LP which is soon to be released.

<u>**exclusive**</u>
a monopoly supplier

MR = Marginal revenue
D = Demand
AR = Average revenue
MC = Marginal cost

*Likely demand for Blot's CD version*

## Questions

**a** Star Enterprise pays Blot a fixed recording contract of £100,000 every time the band records. It is then up to Star Enterprise to determine the price of the tape, record or CD. How much do you think Star Enterprise should sell the CD for if it wishes to make <u>as much profit as possible</u>? (5)

**b** Blot wants Star Enterprise to pay the band a royalty of 10% of Star Enterprise's <u>total revenue</u> from selling Blot's records, tapes and CDs. What price would Blot prefer Star Enterprise to sell the new CD at? (5)

**c** As an economist who is particularly interested in using scarce resources as <u>efficiently</u> as possible and making sure consumers have exactly the 'right' number of CDs, what price would you recommend? (5)

<u>**as much profit as possible**</u>
What is the profit maximising rule? Where MR = MC.

<u>**total revenue**</u>
Where is this maximised? Think of price elasticity of demand.

<u>**efficiently**</u>
Allocative efficiency is where the MC just equals the market price.

# EU farm burden slated

EUROPE'S FARM policy has been condemned as an inefficient, unhealthy and expensive cash-guzzler which costs the average British family nearly £20 per week.

Despite repeated efforts to reform the system which props up European farmers through a system of guaranteed prices, a family of four is still contributing almost £20 every week towards the Common Agricultural Policy through food bills and the rest in extra taxes, states a National Consumer Council (NCC) report.

The latest attack on the £40 billion a year policy follows a warning last week from the Prime Minister that unless the system is reformed it will cost a further £12 billion next year.

The report says that consumers are continuing to pay for an inefficient farm subsidy policy which is failing farmers, harming the environment and damaging the economies of developing countries.

The NCC is demanding new reforms to the system which guarantees farm prices. According to the NCC, farmers in Europe should receive direct payments from their national governments rather than guaranteed prices set at EU level. Each national government would then be able to use taxpayers' money more effectively according to its own needs.

As part of the reforms the NCC would also like to see an end to the limits on farm production currently in use. Such limits tend to keep consumer prices high and make farmers less competitive.

**guaranteed prices**
The guaranteed price is above the national equilibrium price.

**family of four**
Taxpayers support farmers in Europe.

**developing countries**
Cheaper food imports from these nations are kept out by taxes.

(Adapted from the *Western Mail*, 3 October 1995)

## Questions

**a** With the aid of a diagram explain how the Common Agricultural Policy 'props up European farmers through a system of guaranteed prices'. **(5)**

**b** Using your diagram, illustrate how the system might cost the European taxpayer some £52 billion a year. **(5)**

**c** How would a reform of the system to allow national governments to be free to determine their own support systems to farmers enable them to use their taxpayers' money more effectively? **(5)**

**d** Explain how limits on farm production might result in high consumer prices and fewer inefficient farmers. **(5)**

# ICI'S GRAND ACQUISITORS

## Nick Goodway

If you heard of a mergers and acquisitions team that had completed more that 500 deals worth £7.7 billion over the last decade without charging fees, would you hire them, fire them or float them on the stock exchange?

The answer is none of the above. ICI's chairman Sir Denys Henderson might just offer his M&A team a glass of Chablis on their 10th anniversary next month. He might even make sure that the head of the team, John Dewhurst, is on his Christmas card list.

While many of their deals barely register on the M&A Richter scale, the big ones have been Big. In 1984, Sir John Harvey-Jones, former trouble-shooting boss of ICI, ruled that the company was unable to generate enough growth organically. It had to hit the acquisition trail.

Never a man to baulk at a loud tie, it was perhaps not surprising that Harvey-Jones should choose a high-profile route. He appointed David Nash, more recently finance director of Cadbury-Schweppes and now at GrandMet, as the M&A team's first head, while Dewhurst moved in from

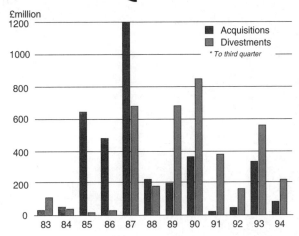

£million

corporate planning as his number two.

In 1984, the team organised the $750 million (£480m) purchase of chemicals concern Beatrice, in 1986 came the $580m acquisition of Glidden paints and in 1987 the $1.95bn purchase of Stauffer. The latter was the biggest deal ICI had ever done and the only involvement by a merchant bank was when Goldman Sachs ran an evaluation of Stauffer's data.

'We save ICI money,' says Dewhurst. 'My team are not paid like merchant bankers.'

The usual measure of M&A charges is called the Lehman Scale. Taking one of ICI's quieter years, 1992, Dewhurst reckons advisers would have charged £15m

fees. His team of five has a budget this year of just £1.25m to cover salaries and travel.

ICI has hard rules. A department chief who has his eye on an acquisition has to put his case to Dewhurst. But life has become tougher. As the chart shows, ICI has moved from a period of acquisitions into one of disposals. Now it swaps assets with its global rivals.

During talks over one of the largest such swaps, with Du Pont, Dewhurst rang Henderson. Using his mobile phone, he intimated that things were not going well. Henderson asked: 'Are you sure you're secure on this line?' 'Yes,' said Dewhurst, 'I'm in the train lavatory and I've locked the door.'

Source: The *Observer*

## Questions

**a** What did Sir John Harvey Jones mean in 1984 when he said that ICI was 'unable to generate enough <u>growth organically</u>'? **(5)**

**b** How would you describe ICI's <u>acquisition</u> of Beatrice in 1984? **(5)**

**c** Using examples explain the economic benefits from internal growth. **(10)**

**d** Why has ICI gone through a period of *divestment* or 'disposals'? **(5)**

**<u>growth organically</u>**
growth from within

**<u>acquisition</u>**
a takeover

# The end of a chapter

THE DISMANTLING of the net book agreement (NBA) and its <u>fixed book prices</u> spells the end of dreams for many aspiring authors as publishers and retailers alike respond to the new competitive market in which they find themselves.

For the big book retailers such as W. H. Smith and Dillons, the ending of the 95-year agreement that propped up book prices is likely to spark a <u>price war</u>.

Books are W. H. Smith's most important product and are likely to be used by the company as a loss-leader to entice customers into the book department and beyond.

Dillons is planning its biggest price promotion slashing the cost of over 200 books ranging from best sellers to specialist titles. Stephen Dunn, the Marketing Director for Dillons, reckons that <u>sales can increase fourfold when prices are cut by just a third</u>. While gross margins must fall for both retailers and publishers the idea is that <u>higher sales</u> will more than compensate.

© Sarah Fairbairn/*The Sunday Times*

**fixed book prices**
keeping book prices up
**price war**
competitive price reductions
**sales can increase fourfold when prices are cut by just a third**
You can calculate price elasticity of demand from this.
**higher sales**
Will sales always rise as price falls? Depends on price elasticity.

(Adapted from the *Sunday Times*, 1 October 1995)

## Questions

**a** What do you understand by the NBA and its *fixed price agreement*? **(5)**

**b** What is the purpose of introducing a 'loss-leader'? **(5)**

**c** Referring to the views expressed by the Marketing Director of W. H. Smith, what is your conclusion concerning the price elasticity of demand for best sellers? How might a price decrease affect overall total revenue in the market for best sellers? **(10)**

**d** How might the possible 'price war' in the book market affect the consumer? **(5)**

# Oil prices fall world-wide

SHELL MAY have been disappointed with the stock market's response to its latest profit figures, but its prediction of cheap oil for at least the next decade is excellent news for the rest of us.

Oil is, literally, the fuel that drives world economic growth and the prospect of it getting cheaper could be enough to usher in another era of prosperity.

John Jennings, Chairman of the Shell UK Division, estimates a trading range of somewhere between $12 and $18 a barrel and firmly believes that 'prices will remain towards the lower end of the range' over the period.

There is little on the horizon to move prices away from this range. The volatility in the oil market largely disappeared once the OPEC producers finally decided that they could no longer hold their oil prices above other non-OPEC producers such as the North Sea and the USA. OPEC has finally admitted that these producers are now too big a force to be contained. The OPEC cartel is now reduced to half-hearted appeals for production sharing, which carry little clout when OPEC itself cannot enforce quotas on its members.

OPEC meetings used to strike terror into western hearts, but this month's affair will merely demonstrate its disarray. It is expected to leave the existing 24.5 million barrels per day ceiling unchanged, ignoring the fact that current production is already 25 million barrels a day. The best that can be hoped for under these circumstances is an increase in demand. This seems unlikely given the trend for milder winters and the increase in non-OPEC oil at lower traded prices.

**stock market's response**
Shell's share price falling – lower profit expectations drive prices down

**drives world economic growth**
Oil is vital as an energy source and raw material.

**OPEC**
Organization of Petroleum Exporting Countries – a cartel of oil producers

(Adapted from the *Daily Telegraph*, 4 November 1995)

## Questions

**a** Explain how cheaper oil might conceivably 'usher in another era of prosperity' in the world economy. **(5)**

**b** Explain how OPEC *used to* operate as a cartel to hold oil prices up. **(5)**

**c** What has caused the decline of the OPEC cartel on world markets? Are there any other factors which might limit the effectiveness of a cartel? **(10)**

**d** Using supply and demand analysis explain how the market price of oil might be affected by each of the following:
  **i** world recession **(3)**
  **ii** a rise in the price of natural gas on world markets. **(2)**

**Data 10**

# Level house prices likely

HOUSE prices are likely to remain in the doldrums until next spring, according to Britain's leading building society.

Even then a significant recovery will only occur if there is a general upturn in consumer confidence and interest rates are not raised again, said the Halifax.

Its comments accompanied news that house prices rose a seasonally adjusted 0.1 per cent in September following a 0.5 per cent fall in August. They are still, however, 0.7 per cent lower than a year ago.

"Generally speaking house prices have remained unchanged since June and are back to their level in August 1993 after peaking slightly in February and March this year," said the Halifax.

Garry Marsh, head of corporate affairs, said he hoped the housing market would show a seasonal pick-up in October.

But he added that weak consumer confidence, continued City speculation about higher base rates and relatively subdued mortgage lending figures, suggested that it would not happen.

Meanwhile separate Bank of England figures showed that overall mortgage lending in August by banks, building societies and other specialised lenders increased only modestly.

Gross lending rose to £4.6bn in August compared with £4.5 bn in July and £4bn last August.

Source: The *Western Mail*

## Questions

a  Using supply and demand analysis, explain how a general 'upturn in consumer confidence' might allow house prices to rise in the future. (5)

b  How would a rise in base rates affect each of the following:
  i  the housing market (5)
  ii  the level of investment in the economy? (5)

c  Apart from interest rates, what other factors might influence the demand for new houses? (10)

**upturn in consumer confidence**
an increase in consumer demand

**base rates**
same as interest rates

13

# Answers

## Data 1: Rightway Electronics PLC

**a** Diminishing returns occurs when the marginal productivity of the variable factor begins to diminish. Marginal production is the extra production which resulted from adding one more unit of the variable factor to the variable factor. It is therefore calculated by:

$$MP_n = TP_n - TP_{n-1}$$

where $MP_n$ refers to the marginal production of the nth worker, $TP_n$ refers to the total production from n workers, and $TP_{n-1}$ refers to the total production from n-1 workers.

The data suggests that diminishing returns sets in after 50 units of capital are used in conjunction with 4 units of materials/workers.

**b** Diminishing returns sets in at some stage due to the imperfect substitution of the variable factors for the fixed factor. Simply, the fixed factor of production, in this case capital, is saturated with the variable factors and total production can no longer increase at an increasing or even a constant rate. At the point where total production begins to increase at a *decreasing* rate, is the point where diminishing returns sets in. The implication of diminishing returns is that marginal production costs will rise.

**c** Increasing the scale of production often results in economies of scale which allow the average production costs to fall as output increases. Rightway Electronics may be able to benefit from the following economies if it increases its scale of production:

- **Financial economies:** Rightway Electronics as a larger enterprise may be able to benefit from loans at preferential rates of interest.
- **Risk-bearing firm:** as Rightway expands it is possible that it may choose to diversify into other areas of production and thus spread its risks. Even if the firm remains committed to manufacturing PCBs market changes in demand and/or supply will have less effect on a larger firm than on a smaller one.
- **Managerial economies:** as the firm expands it can take advantage of specialisation of labour allowing managerial roles to be allocated to specialists in that particular area. Furthermore, bigger firms can buy in management services.
- **Purchasing economies:** as Rightway Electronics increases its scale of production so it can benefit from bulk buying of materials and components which allows the firm to purchase at discounted costs.
- **Technical economies:** as the firm expands it can use some of its existing resources to better advantage – perhaps some machinery is lying idle through part of the working day and this can now be put to full-time use. In addition, specialisation of workers into areas of production most suited to their skills and aptitudes will obviously benefit the firm.

**d** Over expansion might result in diseconomies of scale where the average costs of production begin to rise. The following diagram illustrates the principle of economies and diseconomies and their effect on average production costs.

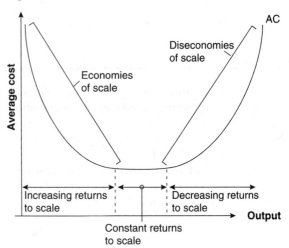

Diseconomies may arise because of the sudden increases in administration costs. There are limits to the efficient functioning of management and as more and more workers are employed by the firm there is often a more than proportionate increase in the managers needed resulting in rising average costs of production.

Further diseconomies might result in the need for very expensive capital equipment to cope with the ever larger production levels.

# Answers

## Data 2: West Midshire Trust Hospital

**a** Health care and education are classified as 'merit' goods by economists. This means that the benefits of these services are not only confined to the person 'consuming' them, but also to society in general. For instance, a vaccination against polio will not only benefit the individual personally, but also society in general as there will be less chance of others catching this disease. Similarly, an individual's education will not only allow him or her to obtain a better job sometime in the future, but will also benefit society in the long term as the individual becomes a productive member of the workforce.

If such services were provided by the normal price mechanism there is a real danger that they would not be consumed in sufficient quantities. Many people would be unable to afford the market price for both health care and education, others would simply prefer to go without. The government therefore allocates these services to the community 'freely' in the form of the NHS and state education.

**b** In the free market, consumer demand and producer supply are brought into line by the price mechanism. If, for instance, the demand for tomatoes is currently greater than the supply of tomatoes at the current market price, then the market price will begin to rise until demand and supply are equal. As price moves upwards consumer demand is choked off whilst, at the same time, producer supply expands – the shortage of tomatoes is removed.

However, there is no price mechanism for NHS operations – there is no automatic mechanism for bringing demand in line with supply for health care services. This means that excess demand for certain NHS services is characterised by waiting lists. In the case of the West Midshire, the waiting list for a simple hip replacement is six months whilst that for a cataract removal is five months.

**c** Opportunity cost refers to the alternative which is lost whenever a choice is made. In the case of the West Midshire, limited resources – doctors, nurses, equipment and medicines – means that a choice has to be made in the provision of hospital services. For example, if the hospital chooses to make more beds available in Accident and Emergency there will be fewer beds available in orthopaedic wards. Likewise, if the hospital chooses to spend money on a scanner there will be less available for physiotherapy.

**d** The government has attempted to increase efficiency and competition in the NHS by encouraging doctors to become fund holders. This means that the doctors are given a certain amount of money per patient and can use that money to purchase services as they see fit. Some practices will choose to spend a greater percentage of their funds on preventative medicine, others will choose to use a greater percentage of their funds on nursing services. However, given the limited funds the doctors must become more cost conscious. Further, doctors are free to purchase the service of hospitals for their patients – they can shop around for the cheapest hip replacement or cataract removal. This in turn will make the hospitals more cost conscious and competitive.

## Data 3: Assembly Techniques Limited

**a** The company currently produces 1,000 boards at a total average variable cost of £4 per board, giving rise to total variable costs of £4,000. In addition, there are fixed costs amounting to £2,000, and therefore the total cost of producing the boards is £6,000. The boards are sold weekly and yield £9,000 in revenue. Therefore the profit to the company per week is £3,000.

**b** The Marketing Director believes that if the price of the boards was increased by 10%, sales would fall by 5%. The price elasticity of demand measures the response of demand to a change in price and is given by:

$$\frac{\text{Percentage change in quantity demanded}}{\text{Percentage change in price}}$$

If the Marketing Director has made accurate estimates, the co-efficient of price elasticity will therefore be $+20 \div -10 = -2$. Demand for the boards is therefore relatively price elastic.

Several factors affect the degree of price elasticity. One major factor is the availability of substitutes in a similar price range. The information given would tend to suggest that Assembly Techniques operates in a market where there are some competitors. Perhaps Assembly Technique gives a similar service to several other companies and so any change in price will have considerable repercussions on sales. Another factor influencing the degree of price elasticity is just how necessary customers view the product. If customers of Assembly Techniques are in desperate need for the boards – perhaps their own production lines will grind to a halt without them – then demand will tend to be price inelastic.

The data provided would tend to suggest that the customers of Assembly Techniques can manage to continue production without this particular PCB. The time factor, indeed, is very important. In the short term, most customers will have little chance to absorb the information and look for alternative supplies if Assembly Techniques was to increase its price. However, in the longer term new suppliers will be sought and demand tends to be relatively elastic.

A final factor influencing the price elasticity of demand is the level of income of the customers. The greater the level of income the more inelastic demand tends to be, and vice versa.

**c** Assembly Techniques has two main options available to it in response to the rent increase of £250:

- It could keep its price and output policy unchanged. Therefore the revenue from sales would still be £9,000, but the total production costs would now rise to £6,250 due to the rent increase. Profits would therefore fall to £2,750. The company would still have spare capacity in the factory and the full increase in costs have been absorbed by a fall in profit.
- It could stimulate sales by reducing the price of the completed board. Currently, the average price of the assembled PCB is £9 (£9,000 ÷ 1,000 boards = £9). A reduction in price by 10% to £8.10 results in an increase in sales from 1,000 boards to 1,200 boards (a 20% increase in sales). These boards will be sold at £8.10 to yield a sales revenue of £9,720. Production costs for these boards will consist of fixed costs of £2,250 (the original fixed costs in total were £2,000) and variable costs which now amount to 1,200 boards × £4 giving a total variable cost of £4,800. Therefore the total production costs amount to £7,050 and Assembly Techniques' profit will be:

$$£9,720 - £7,050 = £2,670.$$

Based on these figures it would be advisable for Assembly Techniques to maintain its existing pricing and output policy rather than reduce the price to stimulate sales. However, this observation is based on the assumption that the variable production costs remain constant at £4 per PCB. If economies in purchasing contracts could be made, it might be possible for the average variable costs to fall and the company might need to review the situation again.

# Answers

## Data 4: Production possibilities: Utopia

**a** A production possibility frontier or curve illustrates the maximum combination of two products which a country/firm/individual is just capable of producing if it uses all its resources in the most efficient manner. By drawing a production possibility curve economists are registering the fundamental principle of economics – that there is a scarcity of resources and hence finished products and services.

The slope of a production possibility curve from left to right illustrates the concept of opportunity cost – that is, as more of one good is made so there is a loss of the other good. In this particular case, the opportunity cost of consumer goods increases as more and more consumer goods are made. Simply, there is an increasing loss of producer goods as the production of consumer goods increases. The cause of this increasing opportunity cost is the fact that resources in general are 'non-homogeneous', meaning that some resources are better suited to one type of work and others are more suited to another. Non-homogeneity of resources results in marginal costs increasing as production increases.

**b** The Utopian government is concerned about current production as represented by position A because either some of Utopia's resources are lying idle or there is full employment but a poor match between resource and area of employment. Either way it is possible to increase production of both consumer goods and producer goods and move to a position of *Pareto efficiency* as indicated by combinations **B** and **C**. Pareto efficiency means that it is impossible to make anyone better off without making someone worse off.

**c** The most suitable growth path for long-term growth will be that represented by AB. This indicates that the government is intensifying the number of producer goods (machines, equipment, transport networks) in the economy. In the long term this 'capitalising' will benefit the economy through the provision of both more producer and more consumer goods.

**d** Combination D is currently unattainable since it is beyond Utopia's production possibility curve. However, it could be possible to reach combination D eventually by either an increase in the availability of resources – perhaps more workers become available from a change in birth and death rates – or the quality of the resources improves. In the case of labour, education and training facilities play a vital role. In the 20th century, technological progress has resulted in very substantial shifts outwards in production possibility curves.

## Data 5: Star Enterprise

**a** Maximum profits occur where the difference between total revenue and total cost is at its (+) greatest. In other words, as production of CDs increases so the addition to total revenue, known as *marginal revenue*, is equal to the addition to total costs, known as *marginal costs*. According to the diagram, profit maximisation will occur at an output of 10,000 CDs with a market price of £7.50.

**b** Blot is obviously interested in its royalties which are a fixed percentage of Star Enterprise's revenue – not a fixed percentage of its profit. Blot therefore wants Star Enterprise to charge a market price which maximises total revenue rather than profits. Maximum revenue occurs when any change in market price is met with an equal and opposite change in market output so as to leave revenue unchanged. This will occur when the price elasticity of demand is –1 and this, in turn, occurs at the mid-point of a downward sloping, straight line demand curve. Therefore, Blot would prefer that Star Enterprise charges £5 for the CDs rather than £7.50.

**c** Economics is a study of how society makes the best use of the scarce factors of production – land, labour, capital and enterprise. An efficient allocation of resources occurs when the market price of the good/service is just equal to the marginal cost of production. Economically, consumers' valuation of the good/service as reflected in the price they are willing to pay is just balanced by the opportunity cost involved in supplying that good/service. This would indicate that consumers want neither more nor less than the amount currently being supplied – the 'right' number is being made available to the market. Given the information in the diagram on page 7, the market price which results in efficient resource allocation is £7.00.

## Data 6: EU farm burden slated

a The Common Agricultural Policy (CAP) is a system of support to farmers in Europe. Its original intention was to ensure that Europe was self-sufficient in farm products, but that original aim has long since been achieved. The system today works by guaranteeing a set price to farmers for their products. Often this guaranteed price is above the natural equilibrium price as shown below.

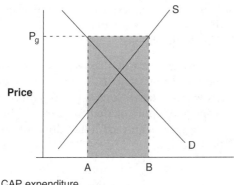

= CAP expenditure
S = Supply; D = Demand

In order to ensure that the market price does not fall below the guaranteed price of $P_g$ the CAP has to purchase the excess supply of AB on the market. This results in the notorious stockpiles throughout Europe.

b In the diagram above, the CAP system has to be prepared to purchase the surplus of AB at the guaranteed market price of $P_g$. Hence the CAP pays out the amount shown in the tinted area of the graph above to the farmers and this ultimately comes from the European taxpayer whose government makes a contribution to the European Union. It has been calculated that the CAP system of support is costing the average British family some £20 per week through guaranteed price support.

c If the CAP system were reformed to allow individual governments the freedom to choose their own methods of support for farmers, then taxpayers' money might be spent more effectively. Some countries might choose to spend less on farming and more, perhaps, on education or the health service, and this might be regarded as being more effective for that particular country. Just as individuals have different priorities, so too have different nations.

The choice of support might also result in more effective use of taxpayers' money. In the CAP system outlined above the taxpayer and the consumer are adversely affected. The taxpayer has to come up with extra money and the consumer never gets the benefit of good harvests. If national governments were to choose other support methods, such as direct subsidies to farmers, then although taxpayers will still have to finance the support at least the consumer will have the benefit of reduced prices.

d Limits on farm production – commonly known as quotas – are a restriction on the supply of farm products able to enter the market. In a free market, the reduced supply will bring about higher consumer prices – simply through the forces of demand and supply. As prices rise so quantity traded in the market place will fall. If demand for the product is sufficiently price elastic the farmers' total revenue will decrease and *unless* costs can be correspondingly reduced, profits will begin to fall. Inefficient farmers with high unit costs will be forced out of business leaving the most efficient farmers with the size to enjoy economies of scale left in the industry.

# Answers

## Data 7: ICI's grand acquisitions

**a** Growth of a company can be generated internally (organically) or externally (through acquisitions and mergers). In the case of organic growth the company attempts to increase its market share/profits/customer base by developing its existing structure and not by acquisition or merger.

External growth through mergers and acquisitions may be a form of vertical integration, in which case the company acquires or merges with another one in the same chain of production but at a different stage. Thus a manufacturer of shoes may take over suppliers of leather. Some take-overs are horizontal integration where one company takes over a similar competitor. Horizontal diversification refers to the situation where one company takes over an entirely unrelated company at the same stage in order spread the risks of production into new areas altogether.

**b** The acquisition of Beatrice in 1984 can be viewed as an example of horizontal integration. ICI is world renowned as a chemical producer and Beatrice, too, is referred to as a chemical concern. Therefore ICI is presumably taking over a competitor.

**c** Internal growth can result in economies of scale which refer to the savings or benefits experienced by a company through increasing its scale of production. Economies of this nature arise because in the long term the company has the option of changing all its factors of production and thus altering its scale rather than its size. Such economies may be financial, for example a larger company with a household name may be able to obtain preferential loans at lower cost than a smaller one. Economies in marketing may also arise as the sales staff are able to cope with larger orders without the need for extra staff. In this area there will also be economies arising from purchasing materials and components in bulk and obtaining discount prices.

Production economies arise as the company adapts its existing resources to meet the extra production required. In any event, there will be little need to increase all the factors of production in proportion to the extra output to be produced. As economies of scale arise so the average cost of making each type of good will diminish.

**d** The divestment or disposals referred to in the data indicate that ICI considers that it has grown too large in some areas and needs to dispose of some of the companies which it has previously acquired. The cause of this could be threefold:

- First, it might be necessary for ICI to realise some of its previous investments back into cash. However, there is no evidence in the data to suggest that this is the case.
- The second cause of the disposals may be that ICI had over-expanded and had run into diseconomies of scale where average costs were beginning to rise. Diseconomies often occur as a result of excessive administration costs.
- The third and most likely factor for ICI is that the acquisition did not turn out as profitably as anticipated and hence the need to 'swap assets' with global rivals. This would make sense if, by swapping, both parties could benefit from further economies of scale.

# Answers

## Data 8: The end of a chapter

**a** In the past, the NBA caused a cartel system to operate in which the prices of books were fixed, usually at above free market levels. The fixed prices allowed both the publishers and the retailers to earn good levels of profit. Competition between book retailers was very limited as retailers were forced to charge the prices set by the NBA.

**b** Loss leaders are a common form of incentive used by retailers to get potential consumers into the shop. A loss leader is an item where the price is set so low, in order to attract custom, that the retailer will suffer a loss on that product. However, the intention is for the customer, once on the premises, to be tempted to visit other areas of the shop and spend on other products, therefore earning an overall profit for the retailer. In this case, cheap books might attract customers into W. H. Smith and they might then visit other departments such as toys and stationery.

**c** The Marketing Director of W. H. Smith is suggesting that the price elasticity for books is considerably elastic. This simply means that a percentage change in the price of the books results in a greater percentage change in the demand for them. In this case, the price elasticity co-efficient for books is suggested to be –12.

$$\frac{\text{Percentage change in quantity demanded}}{\text{Percentage change in price}}$$

$$= \frac{+400}{-33} = -12$$

As a result of this very elastic demand for best sellers, the overall total revenue for W. H. Smith can be expected to rise as prices fall.

**d** A price war consists of competitive book price reductions between the major retailers such as W. H. Smith and Dillons. Obviously, consumers will be beneficially affected by cheaper book prices allowing them to buy more books and/or more other goods and services. However, as price falls, so profit margins on the books will fall and the retailers might be looking for other ways to maintain their overall profits. Perhaps the prices of other products, such as stationery and toys, will rise to compensate for the lower prices on books. Or, the retailer will look for cost savings elsewhere in the business – fewer staff will be employed meaning that customers will have to wait longer to be served. Or, the ordering service will be discontinued as another cost cutting exercise.

# Answers

## Data 9: Oil prices fall world-wide

**a** Oil is a major raw material for many industries and an important energy source for others. Cheaper oil on the world oil markets can only be good news for industry. As costs of production fall so the aggregate supply curve will shift to the right, allowing an expansion of output (and employment) at lower consumer prices. The world economy will move into prosperity as higher incomes result in higher levels of consumer expenditure.

**b** OPEC countries, largely the Middle Eastern oil producers such as Saudi Arabia and Kuwait, operated a price fixing cartel very successfully in the 1970s. By controlling the output of oil to agreed quotas, OPEC effectively held the price of oil at an artificially high level. Unfortunately, world oil consumers in the 1970s had little option but to purchase oil at these inflated prices.

**c** The decline of the OPEC cartel on world markets is largely the result of new oil suppliers entering the market – in particularly North Sea oil producers – who have deliberately undercut the OPEC price. There is now effective competition. Another factor which should be taken into account is a downturn in demand for oil. Mild winters and generally reduced demand as oil substitutes become available have resulted in a natural tendency for world oil prices to fall.

Cartels tend to lose their effectiveness in the long term for a variety of reasons. Their success depends upon persuading everyone to join the cartel and abiding by the rules. Very often members will choose to leave the cartel to sell extra production at cartel prices and hence earn abnormal profits. In the case of OPEC, Nigeria has frequently been the member which failed to abide by the rules. Government intervention of course is another factor which inhibits the effectiveness of the cartel. In the case of OPEC, of course, the cartel is sanctioned by the government.

**d i** A world wide recession will reduce the demand for oil as industry slows down in response to a downturn in consumer demand. The effect on oil prices is illustrated below:

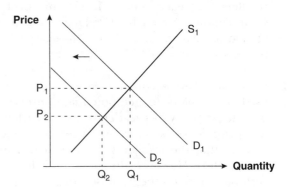

The initial equilibrium price and output is $P_1$ and $Q_1$. The decrease in demand causes the demand for oil to fall to $D_2$ and the resultant new equilibrium is at $P_2$ and $Q_2$. The world price of oil has therefore fallen.

**ii** Natural gas and oil are considered to be substitute forms of energy. This being so, as the price of natural gas rises and hence demand for natural gas falls, so the knock-on effect is for the demand for oil to rise. As the demand curve for oil shifts to the right, so the price of oil will increase on the market, as illustrated below:

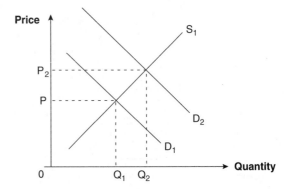

# Answers

## Data 10: Level house prices likely

**a** In the free market the price of a good or service is determined by the interaction of demand and supply. The following diagram illustrates the market for new houses.

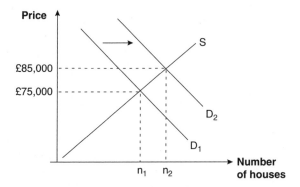

The equilibrium price for these houses is £75,000 if $n_1$ are being bought and sold. If there is an increase in consumer confidence then it implies that consumers feel able to increase their demand for housing – perhaps they feel that their employment prospects are safe and secure, that promotion is around the corner, that the economy is looking brighter, that inflation is under control. . . . As a result, the demand for housing shifts to the right and more houses are demanded at each and every price. The result of this upturn in consumer confidence is that the price of new houses will rise to £85,000 and $n_2$ houses are bought and sold.

**b i** Interest rates affect consumers in the sense that many purchases are undertaken using credit facilities which means that a rate of interest has to be repaid. It is an extra cost to the purchaser. In the case of the housing market, most homes are bought using a mortgage which incurs a rate of interest. If interest rates are rising then it can be expected that the demand for private housing will fall as the costs of mortgage repayments rise. As a result, the fall in demand will cause house prices to fall. However, a further point could be made that higher interest rates will also cause the supply of houses to fall since many builders use overdrafts and loans to survive. As costs rise, the supply of houses will fall and this might ultimately mean that house prices will rise.

**ii** Investment refers to the purchase of capital equipment, tools and other assets for the purpose of increasing productive capacity. At a simple level much investment is undertaken by borrowed money on which a rate of interest has to be paid. Therefore if interest rates are rising so the cost of borrowing increases and the volume of investment is likely to diminish. At a more sophisticated level it could be argued that rising interest rates make it more attractive for companies to maintain their money assets rather than their capital assets. It has to be said, however, that there is increasing evidence that interest rates are only one of several factors influencing the level of investment in the economy. These other factors include the rate of growth of national income and general expectations in the economy as well as previously held stocks of finished goods.

**c** The demand for any good or service is influenced by many factors. In the new housing market the main factor influencing demand will be the price of the house. Generally, as house prices rise so demand can be expected to fall. The availability of mortgages will also influence demand. In the recent past, building societies have been criticised for granting mortgages too readily. Some families have found themselves unable to pay the mortgage when one partner has become unemployed. Therefore mortgage availability is important. Another factor is the price of substitute housing – are second-hand homes much cheaper? What about rented accommodation? The price of related goods when buying a new house must be considered – what is the price of furniture and carpets? The level of one's income must also be considered. When incomes are high and rising the demand for new homes will rise accordingly. Similarly, during a recession when incomes are falling the demand for new homes will fall. Are there any tax incentives for purchasing property? This might cause a change in demand for new houses. Is there consumer confidence that the time is right for buying a new home? In conclusion, there are many factors apart from the rate of interest which should be taken into consideration.

# SECTION B: MAKING PROGRESS

# The route to EMU

The Maastricht Treaty of 1991 established the foundations for the road to full European Monetary Union (EMU) by 1999. The Treaty insists that the <u>budget deficit</u> of participating members in EMU should be within 1% and 3% of gross domestic product (GDP). Evidence (to date) suggests that many European Union members will have a hard job in meeting this requirement (see the diagram below).

**budget deficit**
the difference between government spending and government revenue (in this case spending is more than revenue)

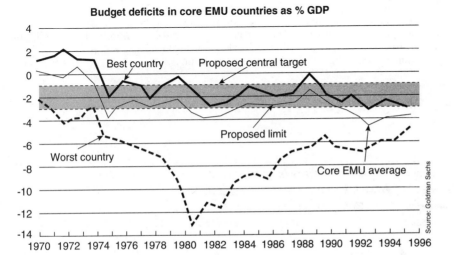

**Budget deficits in core EMU countries as % GDP**

Source: Goldman Sachs

Source: The *Independent*, 20 November 1995

*Budget deficits in core EMU countries*

The main threat, however, to participating countries is the fear that Europe might move wholesale into another <u>recession</u> in the next few years. In the context of low GDP growth rates, a budget deficit of less than 3% of GDP would seem impossible as tax revenues contract and government expenditure is automatically forced to rise.

The only assured route to EMU by 1999 is the route of economic growth and that means low interest rates.

**recession**
falling levels of output, rising unemployment

## Questions

**a** Using the above diagram, explain why many European Union members might have a hard job in achieving a budget deficit of between 1% and 3% of their GDP. **(5)**

**b** Why would a recession tend to cause budget deficits to rise if nothing else changes? **(5)**

**c** What benefits are there economically for the establishment of a single currency (the ECU) in Europe? **(7)**

**d** Explain why low interest rates might result in higher growth in the economy. **(8)**

# Welsh paying through the nose for petrol

WELSH MOTORISTS are paying for the most expensive petrol in the UK. And people living in the sea-side town of Aberystwyth, Dyfed are paying on average 20p more for a gallon of petrol than those in London.

Last night, angry locals in Aberystwyth said the major petrol companies are operating a <u>cartel</u> in the town and attempting to make money out of holiday-makers at the expense of local motorists. Town mayor, Bob Griffin attacked the prices and demanded fairer competition. 'People round here need cars because public transport is scarce. But they are paying extortionate prices,' he said.

However, town council-lors at Aberystwyth believe they have found the answer to the so-called cartel. Numerous planning applica-tions are being considered in the town for supermar-kets who also want to run <u>cut-price</u> petrol stations. The council have indicated that it would look favour-ably at such applications.

**cartel**
an agreement to reduce competition

**cut-price**
where little profit, if any, is made

(Adapted from the *Western Mail*, 5 July 1994)

**How petrol prices compare**

| One litre of leaded four-star petrol at randomly selected garages (Some are run independently from major companies) | SWANSEA | CARDIFF | NEWTOWN | ABERYSTWYTH |
|---|---|---|---|---|
| | TEXACO 55.9p | TEXACO 56.9p | TEXACO 57.9p | TEXACO 59.9p |
| | SHELL 55.9p | SHELL 55.9p | SHELL 57.9p | SHELL 59.9p |
| | BP 53.9p | BP 55.9p | BP 57.8p | BP 59.9p |

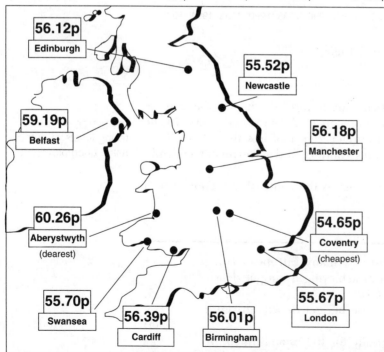

**56.12p** Edinburgh

**55.52p** Newcastle

**59.19p** Belfast

**56.18p** Manchester

**60.26p** Aberystwyth (dearest)

**54.65p** Coventry (cheapest)

**55.70p** Swansea

**56.39p** Cardiff

**56.01p** Birmingham

**55.67p** London

Source: The *Western Mail*

## Questions

**a** In a competitive market with no restrictions or impediments, how should prices be determined? **(3)**

**b** Explain how a cartel for petrol in the Aberystwyth area might be working. **(5)**

**c** Explain how the councillors in the Aberystwyth area propose to break the so-called cartel. **(5)**

**d** In <u>oligopolistic markets</u>, such as that of the retail petrol industry, why is <u>price rigidity</u> very often a market feature? **(6)**

**e** Describe some techniques of non-price competition undertaken in the oligopolistic retail petrol industry. **(6)**

**oligopolistic markets**
where a few large companies dominate the market

**price rigidity**
prices stay constant for long periods

# The developing countries

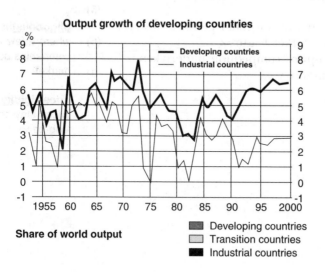

**Output growth of developing countries**

- Developing countries
- Industrial countries

**Share of world output**

- Developing countries
- Transition countries
- Industrial countries

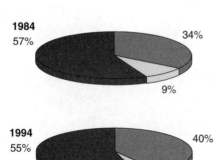

**1984**
57%
34%
9%

**1994**
55%
40%
5%

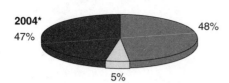

**2004\***
47%
48%
5%

\*estimate

## Questions

**a** Describe the <u>relative trends</u> in output growth between the developing countries and the developed countries.

    **(5)**

**b** By the year 2004 it is expected that the developing nations' share of world output, and hence world trade, will have risen considerably. What reasons can you put forward to explain the growing importance, economically, of the developing nations?

    **(5)**

**c** Although by the year 2004, the recorded <u>gross domestic product (GDP)</u> of the developing nations will be significantly higher than its present level, this does *not* imply that the standard of living of the population will have improved greatly. How would you account for this apparent contradiction?

    **(10)**

**d** The 'transition countries' referred to in the diagram above are the former Soviet Union and the countries of Eastern Europe. What <u>transition</u> is taking place economically in these countries? Explain your answer.

    **(5)**

**relative trends**
increasing, decreasing or level

**GDP**
a measure of output and hence standards of living

**transition**
Think of economic systems.

# An integrated transport system

Stagecoach, the bus operator, is currently in the process of ambitious <u>acquisition</u> plans for the railway industry. Stagecoach already owns South West trains and is likely to bid for all the remaining rail service franchises in the forthcoming rail industry privatisation. The company is already short-listed for the InterCity East Coast and Network South Central franchises.

The company has been fiercely attacked for the manner in which it has built up its <u>market share</u> of the bus sector – it now stands at 17% and the company hopes to reach 25% of the market share in the bus industry, in the near future. The <u>Office of Fair Trading (OFT)</u> has already investigated Stagecoach 24 times and the <u>Monopolies and Mergers Commission (MMC)</u> has, in the past, referred to the company's activities as being 'against the public interest'.

Rail unions fear Stagecoach's plans for staffing levels, but the company are quick to reply that profits will be generated by more passengers rather than less staff.

Certainly, if Stagecoach's plans materialise an integrated transport system is on the cards.

**acquisitions**
takeovers or mergers

**market share**
in this case, the percentage of customers

**OFT**
a government department

**MMC**
a government department

## Questions

**a** What do you understand by the term 'privatisation'? Suggest reasons to explain why privatisation has taken place in the UK economy. **(12)**

**b** What sort of activities undertaken by Stagecoach might have been considered by the MMC to be 'against the public interest'? **(4)**

**c** Why are the rail unions so concerned about staffing levels if Stagecoach manages to obtain rail franchises? **(4)**

**d** If Stagecoach is anxious to generate more profit, do you think that it is a good idea for the company to reduce passenger railway prices? **(5)**

# RATE RISE HANGS ON POUND

CHANCELLOR OF THE Exchequer, Kenneth Clarke, and Eddie George, Governor of the Bank of England, meet at the Treasury on Wednesday to discuss interest rate policy against a background of growing market expectations that base rates will rise in the autumn.

Yet there are few indications of any substantial change in economic outlook since their last meeting in July when they agreed to keep interest rates unchanged. That meeting also took place against a background of market expectations that interest rates would rise.

Since the last meeting output data for the UK economy has suggested that economic growth is slightly stronger than anticipated and bank lending figures show a sharp surge this month. Balanced against this, however, are the figures for both headline and underlying inflation rates, both of which show that the current rate of inflation is well within the lower end of the government's official target range of 1–4%. The statistics for M0 and M4 are also subdued. There is, moreover, a growing belief amongst economists that the trend of consumer spending is beginning to slow down. With signs of a slowing economy and inflation so low, there is not much obvious reason for the Chancellor to opt for a politically embarrassing base rate increase ahead of the October's Conservative Party conference in Blackpool.

Eddie George has argued that when the eventual interest rate increase actually comes it should be a sign of strength rather than of weakness. This is a difficult argument to get across politically for the Chancellor.

The deciding factor about whether there will or will not be a rise in interest rates is likely to depend on the behaviour of sterling.

**base rates**
the rate of interest that the Bank of England charges on loans to the financial system

**economic growth**
a rise in productive capacity of the economy

**M0 and M4**
measures of the money supply: M0 is narrow money; M4 is broad money

(Adapted from The *Observer*, October 1994)

## Questions

**a** What evidence is there to suggest that interest rates will *not* rise following the meeting between the Chancellor and the Governor of the Bank of England? (5)

**b** Explain how the value of the pound might be the crucial factor in determining whether interest rates rise or fall. (7)

**c** What link, if any, is there between the rate of inflation and the level of interest rates? (8)

**d** Distinguish between 'headline' and 'underlying' inflation rates. Why would the government wish to make this distinction? (5)

# Rise of the superpower

# Water and electricity in mega-monopoly mix

A NEW ERA OF MEGA UTILITIES – giant companies supplying water, electricity and gas – is in sight. The first cross-utilities deal moved a step nearer on Friday when North West Water launched a £1.6 billion bid for its local electricity supplier, Norweb.

Open season was launched in the utilities sector after the Trade and Industry secretary, Ian Lang, declined to dispatch the £1 billion offer by Scottish Power for Manweb to the Monopolies and Mergers Commission (MMC).

North West Water, which intends to fund its bid for Norweb by launching a £567 million share rights issue, rushed out its £1.6 billion bid, because of a rumour that an American utility company was interested in buying out Norweb.

The government will come under intense pressure in the next few weeks to halt the takeover frenzy by referring the North West Water bid for Norweb to the Monopolies and Mergers Commission. Jack Cunningham, Labour's Trade and Industry spokesman warned 'The implications for competition, choice and efficiency all need to be examined before we reach the situation where half a dozen huge private monopolies control vast areas of our lives.'

John Redwood, the right-wing Conservative and a firm believer of privatisation, said a unified North West–Norweb could 'gang-up on millions of customers'.

North West Water, not surprisingly, rejects the concerns which are being put forward. Sir Derek Pitcher, the Chairman of North West, believes that a takeover will result in substantial costs being taken out of the two businesses – inevitably resulting in job losses amongst the combined staff of 4000 – and that the benefits will be passed on to water and electricity customers.

**cross-utilities**
two utilities merging together

**monopolies**
large, dominant companies enjoying at least 25% market share

(Adapted from an article by Michael Smith, The *Observer*, September 1995)

## Questions

**a** What is the function of the MMC? (3)

**b** What arguments have been put forward in favour of 'privatisation' of the once state-owned utilities? (8)

**c** Explain in detail the possible concerns expressed by Jack Cunningham in the statement, 'The implications for competition, choice and efficiency all need to be examined before we reach the situation where half a dozen huge private monopolies control vast areas of our lives.' (8)

**d** Explain the argument put forward by the Chairman of North West Water as to how and why the proposed take-over might result in benefits being passed on to consumers. (6)

**competition**
in terms of price, quality and output

**efficiency**
working productively and allocatively

# Potatoes boil as famine fears fuel futures

FEARS THAT current drought conditions will result in severe potato shortages next spring have caused potato prices to treble on the London Commodity Exchange. Contracts for April delivery, the key month for potato futures, closed on Friday at £316 a tonne. Only a week before they were £222 and in mid-June they were a mere £103 a tonne.

A spokesman for Albert Fisher, the produce and food group, commented that 'It is quite clear that the autumn prices of potatoes and other vegetables will be expensive. The problem is the lack of water. Another 10 days of dry weather could prove critical.'

The futures price of £316 a tonne for potatoes next spring compares with a current average delivery price of £115 a tonne. We can expect the price of our humble spud to treble its current price on the commodity markets. How will this tremendous increase affect the consumer?

Many larger trade users of potatoes, including crisp manufacturers, have fixed supply and price contracts with selected growers. They therefore expect to be unaffected by this year's drought. A spokesman for United Biscuits, whose brands include KP Hula Hoops and McCoy's commented, 'All our supplies come from irrigated farms, which ensure quality.'

In the short term, therefore, the consumer should not expect to see potato snacks increase in price substantially. However, the large supermarkets, the fish and chip trade and the wholesale merchants are now engaged in making their futures contracts. These potato users are at the mercy of the current drought and inevitably as potato futures are bid up, so the consumer can expect to take the brunt.

**severe potato shortages next spring**
Demand and supply analysis causes price changes.

**futures**
contracts signed today for delivery in the future

Adapted from an article by Lindsay Vincent, The *Observer*, 13 August 1995)

## Questions

**a** Potatoes, like so many other primary products, are subject to a great deal of price fluctuations compared to the prices of most manufactured products. How do you account for this? **(8)**

**b** With the aid of a diagram explain the current trend for potato prices to increase so substantially. **(5)**

**c** On the basis of the information given, do you think potato snacks such as crisps will hold their current consumer prices? Is there any more information which would be relevant in making your judgement? **(7)**

**d** The box on the right gives the cross-elasticities of potatoes and other products. In each case explain how the expected rise in potato prices will affect the consumption of the other product. **(5)**

**cross-elasticities**
how the price of one good affects demand for another

| Product | Co-efficient |
|---------|--------------|
| Rice    | +1.2         |
| Bread   | +0.9         |
| Meat    | −1.1         |

# DIAMOND DEAL HERALDS A RETREAT FROM THE ABYSS

THE IMMEDIATE threat to the most durable cartel in recent history has passed. This time last week, De Beers, the South African group which for 60 years has organised the cartel of uncut diamond producers was ready to be ripped apart by the departure of one of its most important members – Russia.

De Beers was willing to face the possibility of an all out price war rather than have its London based Central Selling Organisation (CSO) sign yet another worthless contract with Russia.

To the relief of the diamond industry, De Beers instead signed an agreement with Russia that re-established the basic principles of the cartel which controls the supply of uncut diamonds onto world markets. Even when South Africa and the Soviet Union were at opposite ends of the political spectrum, Russian diamonds made their way onto the world market through the De Beers' CSO via a complex web of intermediaries.

The CSO acts as a kind of buffer stock manager for diamond producers in Angola, Australia, Botswana, Namibia, Tanzania and Zaire, as well as Russia and South Africa, and so it controls well over half of world trade in diamonds. It stockpiles uncut diamonds in hard times and releases them when demand is healthy.

Russia formally rejoined the CSO five years ago. De Beers had two main gripes against the Russians. Firstly De Beers said that the Russians were flagrantly breaching its CSO contract by exporting huge quantities of diamonds without using the CSO. Analysts suggest that over $1 billion worth leaked to the west in this way in the last 18 months. Also, as Russia began to build up its domestic diamond cutting, the locals were given the first choice of production, leaving De Beers with the dregs.

The Russians were not happy either. They found it hard to understand that the CSO alone sets the prices. They felt that as big producers they should have some influence over the price. They also suggested that they could get 35% more for their diamonds by selling them outside the CSO.

**cartel**
agreement to reduce competition

**controls the supply**
So what happens to the price?

**stockpiles**
takes the diamonds off the market

**breaching its CSO contract**
Russia ignoring controls on diamond output on world markets

(Adapted from The *Financial Times*, 26 February 1996)

## Questions

a  Explain how the De Beers' CSO operates a cartel in uncut diamonds. **(6)**

b  Why do you think that Russia, in the past five years, has consistently breached its CSO contract? **(6)**

c  What would tend to happen to the cartel agreement and to the market price of uncut diamonds if other countries found large quantities of diamonds which they could mine cost effectively? **(6)**

d  How can you explain the fact that diamonds, a non-essential commodity, command such high prices on world markets whereas water, a essential commodity, commands such a relatively low market price? **(7)**

# Balance of payments accounting

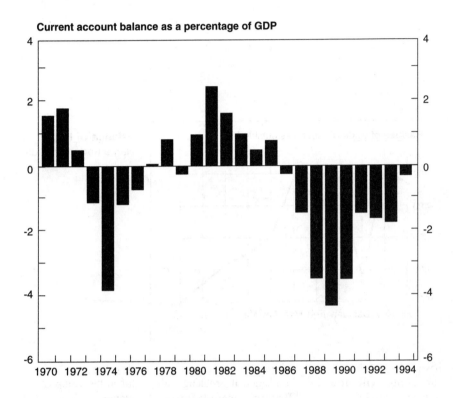

**Current account balance as a percentage of GDP**

Source: *Economic Briefing*, August 1995 (original data from CSO)
*Current account balance*

**Note:** you should consider the importance of the base line shown in the diagram above.

## Questions

**a** What does the 'current account' of the balance of payments
measure? **(5)**

**b** Describe the trend in the current account as shown in the
diagram above. **(4)**

**c** Why is it true to say that the balance of payments will always
balance whatever the state of the current account? **(6)**

**d** If the current account is in a <u>fundamental deficit</u> situation,
evaluate the following alternative policies as a means of
remedying the deficit:
  **i** high interest rates **(5)**
  **ii** depreciation of the value of sterling. **(5)**

**fundamental deficit**
a continuous deficit

# The UK's balance of trade regarding countries outside the EU

Examine the data below:

BRITAIN'S TRADE deficit with countries outside the European Union took a dramatic turn for the worse in August, rising from £872 million in July to £996m.

Stagnating exports and soaring imports have produced a position where the annual rate of deficit has shot up from less than £4 billion in the spring to almost £12bn.

Although the Government maintains that the disappointing exports merely reflect a slowdown in our major overseas markets, there are also grounds for believing that the main benefits of the post-<u>Black Wednesday devaluation</u> have fed through, and that the going will now be tougher.

The higher import figures are put down to this year's rise in industrial investment, but this merely serves to underline the fundamental problem with Britain's manufacturing base – that it cannot provide more <u>investment goods</u> itself.

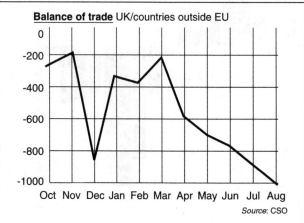

Balance of trade UK/countries outside EU

Source: CSO

**balance of trade**
viable trade in goods

**devaluation**
fall in the value of sterling

**investment goods**
equipment, tools and machinery

Source: The *Observer*, 24 September 1995

**Note:** Black Wednesday refers to the UK's final decision in September 1992 to leave the fixed Exchange Rate Mechanism (ERM) and allow the pound to float downwards and hence be devalued.

## Questions

**a** What do you understand by the term 'trade deficit'? Outline the trend in the trade deficit over the period portrayed in the graph above. **(3)**

**b** Why do you think a devaluation of a currency might result in an improvement in the balance of trade? **(6)**

**c** Why would higher industrial investment in the UK cause an
   increase in the volume of imports? **(2)**

**d** Why is an increase in investment likely to result in an even greater
   increase in the national income of a country than the increase in
   investment which brought it about? **(9)**

**e** Distinguish between *economic recovery* and *economic growth*. **(5)**

# The savings ratio

| Year | Real personal disposable income (£m) | Savings ratio (savings as % of real personal disposable income) |
|------|-----|-----|
| 1983 | 289,000 | 9.7 |
| 1984 | 300,000 | 11.1 |
| 1985 | 310,000 | 10.7 |
| 1986 | 324,000 | 8.7 |
| 1987 | 335,000 | 7.1 |
| 1988 | 355,000 | 5.7 |
| 1989 | 372,000 | 7.2 |
| 1990 | 379,000 | 8.4 |
| 1991 | 380,000 | 10.5 |
| 1992 | 390,000 | 12.8 |
| 1993 | 397,000 | 12.2 |

**Note:** figures are rounded.

Source: *Economic Trends*, CSO, 1995

## Questions

a  What do you understand by the term 'personal disposable income'? **(3)**

b  How far would you agree that personal savings is a direct function of personal disposable income? **(5)**

c  What other factors will affect the volume of personal savings in the economy? **(10)**

d  What economic effects might there be if there is a sharp decrease in the personal savings ratio? **(7)**

# Measuring inflation

Consider the following table which shows the price changes of selected items over a one-year period in Utopia.

| Commodity | Percentage average price change | Percentage of consumer expenditure spent on this commodity on average |
|---|---|---|
| Food | +10 | 40 |
| Public transport | 0 | 10 |
| Entertainment | +5 | 5 |
| Energy/fuel | −5 | 15 |
| Housing | +2 | 20 |
| Household durables | +10 | 5 |
| Other | −1 | 5 |

### The Smiths

Fred and Rita Smith are retired and live in a small village in a rural region of Utopia. They live on a small occupational pension from Fred's previous job and the state pension which is fixed annually in November. They do not own a car and buy most of their daily provisions from the local shop. Most of their income is spent on food and energy/fuel.

### The Forsyths

Penny and Charles Forsyth are in their mid-thirties and live in a fashionable suburb of the capital city of Utopia. They have no children and their combined income is in the region of £65,000. Penny and Charles often dine out and spend a higher than average proportion of their income on entertainment of various sorts including foreign travel. Penny and Charles are able to save a considerable amount of their combined income – mostly in the form of purchasing equity shares in blue-chip companies.

## Questions

a  Calculate the average rate of inflation from the information given, showing your working. **(10)**

b  Do you think that the measured rate of inflation is a good indicator of the personal inflation rate facing each of these couples? **(15)**

# TORIES PLAN U-TURN ON CAR CULTURE

**EXCLUSIVE**

Polly Ghazi
*Environment Correspondent*

TRANSPORT Secretary Brian Mawhinney has given a clear signal that the Government is preparing a dramatic U-turn on road building, reversing a decade of policy.

In his first full interview since taking office, Dr Mawhinney signalled that, for the first time since the war, the Conservatives have turned away from unfettered car ownership – what Baroness Thatcher famously described as 'the great car economy'.

The development may effectively spell the end of the Government's £19 billion road-building programme, which has aroused violent opposition across the country. The beginning of the end could come as early as next month, when the programme is likely to be savaged in the Budget by Chancellor Kenneth Clarke, who is desperately seeking to cut public spending.

Dr Mawhinney used his interview with *The Observer* to issue an invitation to the environment lobby to present him with concrete ideas on how to shape a new transport policy for Britain.

'"The great car economy" is not a phrase I have chosen to use in my first 10 weeks in this job – nor do I envisage using it in the future . . . I am happy to talk in detail to the green lobby about how they see transport policy developing and ask them how, for example, the Government could persuade people to get out of their cars and use public transport.'

Dr Mawhinney, who could only embark on such a significant change of direction under the instruction of the Prime Minister, is understood to have launched a wide-ranging review of the motorway-building programme that will include a number of schemes deeply unpopular with Tory MPs, such as widening the M25 to 14 lanes in Surrey.

In his interview he also spoke positively of measures to control traffic such as cutting speed limits and restricting rush-hour access to busy roads.

While emphasising that the car had 'brought great freedom and choice to the British public', he added that managing traffic rather than building roads was the way forward. And he hinted that he may scrap unpopular road schemes through open countryside and wildlife habitats.

'Environmental concerns about transport are obviously taking a higher priority in people's minds . . . and we must address these better over the next decade,' Dr Mawhinney said. 'I want to look with particular care at schemes that have major environmental sensitivities.'

Dr Mawhinney's remarks confirm speculation that the Cabinet is embarking on a fundamental rethink of transport policy. Earlier this year Environment Secretary John Gummer warned that rising traffic levels were stifling cities and towns and that 'the car must become our servant rather than our master'.

At the time he appeared to be a lone voice. But events are now conspiring to push the Government towards a greener roads policy. With the general election less than two years away, Conservative MPs in the South-East of England are vociferously opposing the M25 and other motorway widening schemes. Smog alerts this summer have heightened public anxiety over the link between car fumes and asthma. And in two weeks' time, the influential Royal Commission on Environmental Pollution will publish a devastating assault on the Government's transport policies. The report will urge Ministers to halt the £19bn roads programme, put up to 13p extra on a gallon of petrol and massively increase investment in public transport.

Source: The *Observer*

## Questions

a Give reasons to suggest why the government may reduce the current road building programme. **(5)**

b Suggest two alternative policies which the government could use to persuade car owners to use public transport. **(15)**

c In Singapore, the government introduced a pricing policy in the form of licences for car owners wishing to take their cars into the city centre. The aim was to encourage car owners to use public transport or at least car share. What would tend to determine the success of such a policy if it were to be introduced into our major cities? **(5)**

# Minister condemns EU over tobacco farm aid

**By David Fletcher**
Health Services
Correspondent

A ROW erupted between Britain and the European Commission yesterday over subsidies to tobacco growers.

Tom Sackville, the junior health minister, said it was hypocritical to pay the farmers millions of pounds while trying to discourage smoking.

The attack came at the start of Europe Against Cancer week, a commission initiative to increase awareness of the disease, cut down smoking and promote healthier lifestyles.

The commission condemned Mr Sackville for diverting attention from the purpose of the week and seeking party political advantage at the start of the Conservative Party conference.

Mr Sackville said Brussels had double standards. He claimed that it was promoting anti-smoking campaigns while spending several hundred million pounds a year supporting the production of tobacco by farmers in Greece and six other EU member states.

Britain had one of the best records in Europe for cutting smoking, he said. But it was still criticised by the EU for opposing a ban on tobacco advertising.

Smoking in Britain was discouraged with high levels of taxation on a packet of 20 cigarettes – £2.11 compared with 46p in Spain – and by raising the price by three per cent above inflation each year.

The Government also had an effective voluntary agreement with the tobacco industry to limit advertising and to prevent promotions in magazines for young people or near schools.

"While we pile on taxes on tobacco in this country, some of those taxes are being spent in Europe to subsidise tobacco farmers," Mr Sackville said. "That is ironic and it is unsatisfactory."

He said the EU subsidised farmers with almost £3 million a day to produce tobacco that was dumped on international markets "to clog the arteries of the Third World".

The subsidies were an extreme example of inappropriate use of taxpayers' money. "What we need is a European-wide harmonisation of tobacco taxation if we are to have a European-wide smoking policy," Mr Sackville said.

Geoffrey Martin, UK head of the European Commission, said the subsidies to tobacco growers were being reduced. But it was better to support the farmers than throw thousands out of work.

He said EU governments, including Britain, had agreed on this support while tobacco farmers switched to alternative crops. Mr Sackville's attack was an apparent attempt to gain party political advantage.

According to EU figures, Europe is the second largest producer of cigarettes in the world after China. It is also the world's biggest exporter with 218 billion cigarettes sent abroad in 1993.

The Department of Health said smoking in Britain had fallen by 28 per cent since 1980, the biggest fall in any EU country except Holland.

● Women are ignoring advice that smoking causes cancer and more are dying from the disease than before, says a report published yesterday.

Doctors, health boards and hospitals are unsure what to do to reverse the trend, adds the report by the Government and the Cancer Research Campaign. It gathers information on new cases and deaths to show that Scotland has the highest rates of lung cancer in the world.

The number of men with the disease is falling, but the number of female victims has risen fourfold over 30 years.

---

### TAX ON SMOKING

How the tax component of the price of a packet of 20 cigarettes varies widely between EU countries:

|  | Price | Total tax |
|---|---|---|
| Denmark | £3.37 | £2.80 |
| Finland | £2.92 | £2.21 |
| Ireland | £2.83 | £2.15 |
| Britain | £2.74 | £2.11 |
| Sweden | £2.63 | £1.82 |
| Germany | £2.32 | £1.63 |
| France | £2.14 | £1.60 |
| Belguim | £2.12 | £1.58 |
| Austria | £1.87 | £1.38 |
| Holland | £1.83 | £1.32 |
| Luxembourg | £1.54 | £1.05 |
| Greece | £1.39 | £1.01 |
| Portugal | £1.18 | 96p |
| Italy | £1.27 | 92p |
| Spain | 65p | 46p |

Source: The *Western Mail*, 10 October 1995

## Questions

**a** Explain how the British government is seeking to reduce smoking. What constraints do you think there might be on the success of these methods? (8)

**b** What argument can be put forward to explain why smoking by individuals represents a misallocation of scarce resources? (7)

**c** Explain, with the aid of a diagram, how the EU 'subsidised farmers with almost £3 million a day to produce tobacco that was dumped on international markets to clog the arteries of the Third World.' (10)

# Government finances

EVERYTHING HAS its price. Like us, if a government wants to spend more it has to earn more through taxes, or borrow more, or dip into savings (which governments do not really have).

Cutting taxes – as the government wants – means the choice is between less spending, more borrowing, or a combination of the two.

Borrowing is far from ideal. If the government is borrowing from us there is less of our money available for private industry to borrow. This will have an impact on private sector investment and ultimately economic growth in the future. On top of that the more the government borrows from us, the higher the interest rate offered to us and this will have repercussions on employment levels and possibly the external value of the pound.

Interest rate payments on the national debt (the total of all outstanding government borrowing) already runs at £25 billion a year – almost as much as the cost of the NHS. A year ago, the government forecast that its borrowing for this financial year would be £21.5 billion. The estimate has risen to £23.5 billion, but many analysts are talking about a final public sector borrowing requirement (PSBR) of about £26 billion.

Despite this obvious deficit in the government's finances, the Chancellor still says that his ultimate aim is to balance the government's budget by the end of the decade. Given the Chancellor's desire to reduce the PSBR and to decrease taxes, there will be little option but to reduce government expenditure.

**Income and expenditure** 1995–96 *(£billion)*
Projected as of November 1994 budget

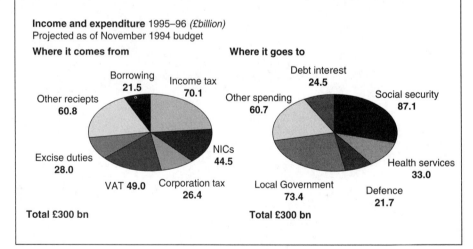

**Where it comes from**

- Borrowing **21.5**
- Income tax **70.1**
- Other reciepts **60.8**
- Excise duties **28.0**
- VAT **49.0**
- Corporation tax **26.4**
- NICs **44.5**

**Total £300 bn**

**Where it goes to**

- Debt interest **24.5**
- Social security **87.1**
- Other spending **60.7**
- Health services **33.0**
- Local Government **73.4**
- Defence **21.7**

**Total £300 bn**

(Adapted from The *Observer*, 28 November 1995)

# Questions

**a** Explain how government borrowing from the private sector will eventually result in lower economic growth in the future. (8)

**b** Explain how interest rate rises might affect the following:
   **i** the level of employment (5)
   **ii** the external value of the pound. (5)

**c** What is the true cost to the economy of continual government borrowing? (5)

**d** What is meant by a 'balanced budget' as proposed by the Chancellor? (2)

# Answers

## Data 11: The route to EMU

**a** The evidence in the graph provided on page 27 suggests that many EU members will have difficulty in achieving the criteria of a 1–3% of GDP budget deficit before full monetary union in 1999. The average deficit for core EMU members has often been outside the maximum of a 3% of GDP limit during the period 1970 to 1995 and the worst country has been consistently outside the maximum limit – reaching a 13% of GDP budget deficit in 1980.

**b** A recession is characterised by falling GDP and rising unemployment levels. As a result, the government spending on benefits for the unemployed will automatically rise whilst, simultaneously, the revenue from income tax will fall. The budget will almost certainly go into deficit. In addition, discretionary fiscal policy undertaken by the government will add to the deficit as the government seeks to stimulate the economy by public spending programmes such as new schools and transport networks.

**c** There are several recognisable benefits from the introduction of a single currency. First, transaction costs involved in the current export and import business across Europe will diminish very substantially. This will ultimately mean cheaper products for European consumers. Secondly, destabilising currency speculation in European currencies will be pointless – although there will be room for speculation between the ECU and other world currencies. Thirdly, European economies will almost certainly be tied to the strong German economy and will therefore benefit from low inflation and interest rates. Finally, a strong EMU with a strong ECU will create a world economy to compete with the strong world economies of America and Japan.

**d** Low interest rates are often regarded as necessary for future economic growth. For one thing, low interest rates cause consumer demand to expand since many purchases are undertaken with borrowed money. As consumer demand picks up, so industry must respond with increased output. However, many economists would regard this as *recovery* in the economy rather than *growth* in the economy.

Economic growth is associated with an increase in the productive potential of the economy which then allows the production possibility curve to shift outwards. The major cause of economic growth is investment in the form of improved technology, equipment and machinery. Producer investment is inversely related to the level of interest rates in the economy: the lower the interest rate the higher the level of investment. The diagram below refers to the marginal efficiency of capital (MEC) curve.

The MEC is a measure of the rate of return on successive units of capital. As a company employs more and more capital so the rate of return diminishes. How many machines should it employ given that the market rate of interest is R%? The answer is $X_1$ machines: any fewer and it would be possible to improve returns by employing more machines; any more and it would be possible to improve returns by keeping assets in an interest-bearing financial form.

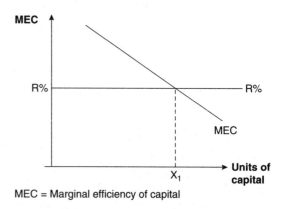

MEC = Marginal efficiency of capital

*The marginal efficiency of capital curve*

### Data 12: Welsh paying through the nose for petrol

**a** In a competitive market with no restrictions or impediment the prices of goods and services are determined by the market forces of demand and supply. Consumer demand and producer supply establish an equilibrium price and quantity traded, as illustrated in the diagram below:

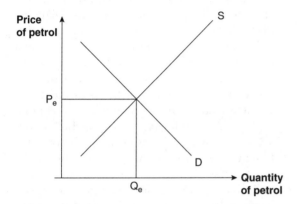

The demand for petrol varies inversely with its price whilst producer supply varies directly.

At price $P_e$, the quantity which consumers are willing to buy is just equal to the quantity which producers are willing to supply and the market is in equilibrium. Changes in the demand or supply curve will trigger off changes in equilibrium price and quantity.

The competitive nature of the free market should ensure that marginal production costs are very close to consumer prices and this would indicate that consumers want neither more nor less of the good in question. In other words, the free competitive market will ensure allocative efficiency of the scarce resources.

**b** In the Aberystwyth area the cartel referred to would seem to be some form of agreement between the major petrol companies to set their pump prices at an agreed level rather than competing price-wise to attract custom. Holiday makers in the area would tend to have a price inelastic demand for petrol and are prepared to purchase the petrol at the inflated prices suggested by the councillors. Of course, local residents who are very dependent upon private transport have to pay the same inflated prices.

**c** The councillors are proposing to break the cartel by introducing more competition into the area in the form of large supermarkets. Such supermarkets are willing to supply petrol as part of their overall service at cut-prices. The other petrol companies will have to follow suit if they hope to maintain their market share and the cartel will break.

**d** Oligopolistic markets are characterised by a small number of companies each producing a similar but not identical product or service. Prices in such markets tend to be rigid or stable for quite long periods of time. The reason for this is that each company recognises that it is not independent from the actions of its competitors. If one of them chooses to increase its price, then there is the fear that competitors will not follow suit. As a result, it will lose market share to competitors. On the other hand, a price reduction by one company will probably result in competitive price reductions as each company cuts price to maintain its market share. This is known as a 'price war' and in the end it is possible for some companies to be forced out of business. This nervousness about price changes and the possible reactions which might be evoked create a rigidity in the market.

**e** Since price competition is so limited in oligopolistic markets, firms have to find other ways of competing – unless they form a cartel which covers not only price fixing, but other forms of competition too. Petrol stations typically engage in non-price competition in the area of free gifts and vouchers. Also the stations engage in competition in the form of opening hours and non-petrol products available.

# Answers

## Data 13: The developing countries

**a** The data indicates that the developing countries have consistently higher growth rates compared to their industrialised neighbours over the period 1955–95. The only exception to this is for a very short period in the late 1950s. Both developed and developing nations' growth paths are similar in the sense that they generally rise and fall together. It is, however, noticeable that the difference between growth rates is actually rising and by the year 2000 the developing nations could have a growth rate of more than 3% above that of the industrialised nations.

**b** The growing importance of the developing countries – particularly those in the so-called Pacific Rim – can be explained by several factors. First, these countries have received large amounts of inward investment in the form of multi-national companies. Such companies help to provide local infrastructure on which economic growth is dependent. Secondly, such countries are less burdened with red tape and bureaucracy which tend to stifle growing businesses. Perhaps the most essential feature which enables developing countries to grow at such high rates is the low unit labour costs. This allows these countries to obtain a high degree of competitiveness against industrialised nations whose labour forces are organised and inflexible to wage cuts. Finally, the increased share of world trade which developing countries are now enjoying can be partly explained by the fact that they are producing quality products at competitive rates. Investment in production methods and on-the-job training has resulted in substantial economies of scale which allow these nations to increase their world share of the market.

**c** Although the measured GDP in the developing countries can be expected to rise significantly by 2004 it does mean to say that every resident will have an improved standard of living. For one thing, it is more relevant to examine the per capita GDP rather than the absolute level of GDP so that some acknowledgement can be taken of population changes. In relation to this, some recognition must be made that although some people will be very much better off, others will be no better off and possibly worse off. Very often the benefits of economic growth are confined to a small proportion of the population. Standards of living also depend upon factors such as the length of the working week and the condition under which people are working. If the working week is long and condition at work are poor, then despite a rise in GDP, it is misleading to assume that standards of living have improved. Reference, too, has to be made to the general price level. GDP must be measured at constant prices in order for a true reflection of standards to be assessed. If GDP is measured without reference to changing price levels then it is very possible to over-assess or under-assess standards of living. Finally, some consideration should be made of the adverse externalities imposed by growth – pollution, de-forestation, congestion. Each of these will have some bearing on the standard of living of the population.

**d** Transition economies are economies which are in the process of changing their economic systems from a centrally controlled (command) economy to a free market economy. In the former, the state undertook the essential task of deciding what should be made, how many and in some cases who would receive the goods and services once made. The problems which arose have been well documented – lack of consumer choice, inefficiency of industry since the profit motive for production was missing, lack of motivation for workers and so on. The transition to a market economy allows the price mechanism, working through consumer demand and producer supply, to solve the fundamental economic problems of what to make, how much and who will obtain the goods and services once produced. The free market gives free choice to both consumers and producers who are individually motivated to maximise utility and profits respectively. Transition economies struggle to cope with high inflation rates and unemployment during the transitional period.

# Answers

## Data 14: An integrated transport system

**a** Privatisation refers to the sale of government owned assets to private owners. There have been two spates of privatisation: 1979–84 when the government sold its holding in several organisations which already had competition in the private sector; and 1984 onwards when the government sold state-owned monopolies into the private sector. In many cases, the monopoly status remained and thus the need for industry 'regulators' in the form of OFTEL, OFGAS, OFWAT and so on.

Privatisation should be regarded as one arm of 'supply side economics' which aims to create a framework of conditions which increases competition and efficiency in markets so as to cause the aggregate supply curve of the economy to shift rightwards, thereby reducing price levels whilst simultaneously stimulating output and hence employment opportunities. This is illustrated below:

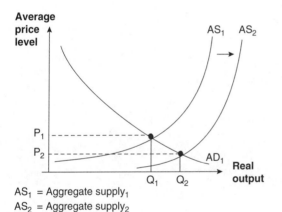

AS$_1$ = Aggregate supply$_1$
AS$_2$ = Aggregate supply$_2$
AD$_1$ = Aggregate demand$_1$

The main point put forward for privatisation is that by freeing industry from state ownership and control forces the industry to operate competitively and thereby increases efficiency. The newly created PLCs must provide dividends for shareholders or suffer the consequences. This means that productive and allocative efficiency must improve.

In addition, of course, privatisation gave the government the opportunity to reduce the need for a public sector borrowing requirement (PSBR) for expenditure purposes. Privatisation yielded billions to the Exchequer.

One very important motive behind privatisation was the attempt to generate a nation of shareholders who would dip their toes into privatisation shares before splashing out in other share buying waters. By channelling funds directly into companies in this manner it was hoped that UK investment levels would increase, and with it, economic growth. Unfortunately, evidence suggests that although share ownership has widened it has not deepened.

**b** The MMC is trusted with the right to investigate monopolies and to restrict mergers both which might be 'against the public interest'. In the case of Stagecoach, the MMC might be particularly interested in its pricing policy and the quality of service to customers. If Stagecoach has few competitors in a certain area, it might be that the company has been seriously 'overcharging' and/or operating an infrequent, unreliable and potentially unsafe service.

**c** If Stagecoach succeed in obtaining rail franchises then presumably the company will be anxious to generate profit from its investment. It is therefore a possibility that the company will seek to reduce the costs of providing the rail service. Although many costs are fixed, it might be possible to reduce manning levels in the rail industry; hence the rail unions' concern.

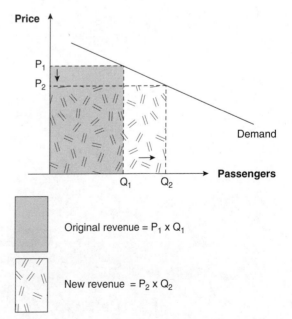

Original revenue = P$_1$ × Q$_1$

New revenue = P$_2$ × Q$_2$

**d** Stagecoach might seek to increase profitability by increasing its revenue rather than by decreasing its costs. One way to do this might be to reduce rail passenger prices with the aim of encouraging more passengers 'to take the train'. The success of this price move will depend essentially on the price elasticity of demand for rail travel. Only if demand is relatively price elastic will a reduction in fares bring about a substantial rise in passengers which will be necessary for increasing profits, assuming costs remain fairly constant. This is illustrated above.

## Data 15: Rate rise hangs on pound

**a** First, since the previous meeting in July there had been no substantial change in the economy – the rate of interest was left unchanged in July and therefore there is a strong possibility that interest rates would be left unchanged in October. Secondly, there were signs that economic growth was slowing and any increase in the rate of interest would slow growth even more as household consumption and producer investment fell in response to higher interest rates. Finally, there was no justification for increasing interest rates on the inflation front as the current rate of inflation was well within the target level of 1–4%.

**b** The value of sterling might be the crucial determinant of whether the Chancellor finally ends up increasing the rate of interest in the economy – the base rate. Interest rates have a recognised effect on the value of a currency. If the pound is weak against other currencies the Chancellor may well resort to putting up the base rate. High interest rates in the UK will make sterling look relatively attractive and 'hot' money chasing high rates of interest will flow into the UK. Therefore the demand for sterling will rise and so its international value will rise accordingly.

**c** High interest rates are usually regarded as an effective anti-inflationary policy. Inflation is often the result of excessive demand in the economy and any policy which can control demand will have the benefit of reducing the rate of inflation. Since much consumer and producer expenditure is undertaken with borrowed money, high interest rates will ultimately have the effect of dampening these two forms of expenditure and hence reducing the rate of inflation. There is, of course, an opportunity cost in using high interest rates. First, the repayment of interest on the national debt will increase along with base rates and, secondly, reduced expenditure in the economy is often associated with rising levels of unemployment.

**d** Headline inflation includes mortgage interest repayments whilst underlying inflation excludes such repayments from the calculation of the rate of inflation. The differentiation arises because higher interest rates are often used as an anti-inflationary measure and although obviously useful, will have the effect of raising the recorded headline rate of inflation. The government might wish to distinguish between headline and underlying because politically, underlying inflation might be more attractive to the electorate when interest rates are high.

# Answers

## Data 16: Rise of the superpower

**a** The MMC is a government department whose general aim is to investigate market situations which might be 'against the public interest'. The MMC, on referral from the Office of Fair Trading and/or the Secretary for Trade and Industry, may be asked to investigate companies, industries or organisations, report back and make recommendations if there is a suspicion that unfair trading might be prevalent. The bodies investigated must be within the working definition of a monopoly, ie possess a market share of more than 25%.

The MMC can also be asked by the Secretary for Trade and Industry, to investigate proposed or actual mergers between companies if there is a threat that the merger will result in commercial trading which 'is against the public interest'. The criteria for 'public interest' will include pricing, quality of service, choice and efficiency. Should the MMC rule that the merger is against the public interest then it can be prevented from occurring.

In the data provided, the bid by North West Water for Norweb had not been referred to the MMC for investigation, but pressure was put on the Secretary for Trade and Industry to make such a referral.

**b** The arguments put forward for privatisation of the once state-owned utilities are many. First, privatisation forces the industry to become much more cost-conscious and efficient since government support in the form of taxpayer's money can no longer be used to prop up inefficient industries. In macro-economic terms, privatisation and the resultant improvement in competitiveness and efficiency will cause the aggregate supply curve to shift rightwards, therefore leading to more output at lower rates of inflation.

A second argument in favour of privatisation concerns investment funds. It was hoped that privatisation would stimulate an interest in direct share buying by individuals who would normally channel their savings into banks, unit trusts and building societies. This direct investment in industry was hoped to be both long-term and deepening with time. In practice, privatisation appears to have widened share ownership, but not deepened it.

Privatisation has also allowed the government to reduce marginal tax rates, such as pay as you earn (PAYE) income tax and corporation tax, without increasing the public sector borrowing requirement (PSBR). In fact the PSBR actually became a PSDR – a public sector debt repayment – in the mid 1980s. Lower marginal tax rates are intended to create an incentive to work and to invest in industry – again causing the aggregate supply curve to shift to the right.

**c** The Labour Party's Trade and Industry spokesman was concerned that allowing one utility monopoly to take over another utility monopoly would have serious implications for competition, choice and efficiency. Allowing the creation of forever bigger and bigger monopolies which then have the power to control basic utilities such as water, electricity, gas and so on reduces competition and choice in the market which privatisation sought to increase. In *local* areas consumers would be forced to purchase their basic utility requirements from the one huge 'superpower' which could well abuse its monopoly position.

In terms of efficiency there is a very real danger that huge monopolies will be very much resource inefficient and charge consumers prices which are well above the marginal production costs. Resource efficiency takes place when price and marginal costs are equal implying that consumers want no more and no less of the product. Such a situation is most likely in competitive markets.

**d** The Chairman of North West Water is most likely referring to the economies of scale which might result from the merger. Economies of scale – perhaps savings made in bulk buying of materials – will result in lower average production costs which might then allow the organisation to pass on the benefits to the consumer in the form of lower prices. However, the *Observer* journalist is also keen to point out that costs will be more likely to fall as a result of redundancies rather than economies of scale.

## Data 17: Potatoes boil as famine fears fuel futures

**a** Primary products such as potatoes are often subject to severe price fluctuations over a comparatively small time scale, whereas the price of manufactured products, such as cars and TVs, often remain stable for several months at a time. Why this difference in price stability? The answer is twofold.

First, primary products are very much influenced by non-human forces in the shape of the weather and disease. Farmers may plan to harvest X tonnes of potatoes next year and plant accordingly, but a severe drought such as that mentioned in the data can result in a very different outcome. Manufacturing industry has a much more controllable output level. If a car manufacturer plans and has the resources to produce X cars next month, then there is little to cause a deviation from that plan. The supply curve for primary products is very unstable and each shift will result in a new market price. Conversely, the supply curve for manufacturing cars is much more static creating a much more stable price level.

Secondly, both the demand and supply curves for primary products tend to be price inelastic resulting in a steep demand and supply curve. As a result, a change in either demand or supply will cause a large adjustment in the price. The demand and supply of manufactured products tends to be more price elastic with less steep demand and supply curves. In this case, a change in either demand or supply conditions will only cause a small adjustment in equilibrium price.

The diagram below left illustrates the effect of a shift in demand for primary products.

Since farm products are planted only once or twice a year there is, generally, a fairly fixed supply available and even fairly large price changes do not bring about major changes in output. Supply is price inelastic.

Similarly, farm products, in general, are essential in our lives and we are willing to pay more for our food in order to obtain it. Demand is price inelastic.

In this case, an increase in the demand for the product brought about by a shift in the demand curve from $D_1$ to $D_2$ will cause a large adjustment in price from $P_1$ to $P_2$.

**b** In the diagram below right the initial price of potatoes before the current drought is given by $P_1$. This market price is established by the interaction of demand and supply as represented by $D_1$ and $S_1$. The water drought subsequently causes the supply of potatoes to fall to that represented by $S_2$ and the result is for the natural equilibrium market price for potatoes to rise to $P_2$.

**c** The information presented tends to imply that although the price of potato snacks such as crisps will remain unaffected in the short term since manufacturers have already established their contract prices in the past, in the long term the price of such snacks can be expected to rise. Unless the potato futures market returns to similar prices ruling prior to the drought it must be expected that at some time in the future potato snack manufacturers such as United Biscuits will have to undertake new

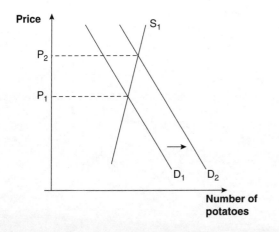

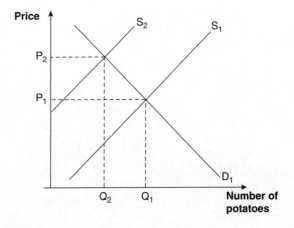

contracts at higher costs to themselves. Although they may be able to absorb some of the extra production costs in reduced profit margins, it is extremely likely that the manufacturers will choose to pass some of their higher production costs onto the consumer in the form of higher retail prices – especially as other potato users such as supermarkets and fish and chip shops will have already taken a similar route. However, further information might reveal that the price of substitute snacks such as crisps and fruit might be decreasing and therefore in the long term consumers might turn their attention to these snacks, causing the demand for potato-based snacks to fall and ultimately allowing price to remain constant or even fall. It would also be interesting to have further information such as trends in sales of potato-based snacks.

The question seems to be looking at a snap shot of the potato snack market and trends in demand over a number of years might result in different conclusions.

It is worthwhile considering the market power of these potato snack manufacturers. The data provided seems to suggest that their sheer size already enables them to make attractive contracts with the potato suppliers – 'fixed supply and price contracts' and 'all our supplies come from irrigated farms, which ensure quality' are quotes that support this. In such a situation, the potato users may have the market power to reduce the price hike of the potatoes. In other words, they force the growers to put up with the problems (and the financial implications) caused by the drought.

**d** Cross-elasticity of demand measures the degree to which the quantity demanded of one good is affected by changes in the price of another good. In this case, what happens to the demand for rice, bread and meat when the price of potatoes goes up?

The cross-elasticity coefficient is given by the formula:

Percentage change in demand for good X
——————————————————————————————
Percentage change in price of good Y

Where two goods are substitutes, as the price of one rises so the demand for the other will increase and this will give rise to a positive cross-elasticity co-efficient. In contrast, where two goods are complementary a rise in the price of one will cause a fall in the demand for the other – the coefficient will be negative.

The information provided therefore suggests that rice and bread are substitutes for potatoes whilst meat complements potatoes.

# Answers

## Data 18: Diamond deal heralds a retreat from the abyss

**a** The CSO which is organised by the De Beers group operates a cartel by controlling the quantity of uncut diamonds which enter the market place. In this manner, the CSO can control the market price for uncut diamonds. The CSO acts as a buffer stock agent for the cartel members. Presumably, the CSO decides a guaranteed price for cartel members for the diamonds. In bad years, when there is a lack of demand for the diamonds and when, as a result, the market price is falling below the guaranteed price, the CSO will buy up and stockpile excess diamonds creating an artificial shortage and hence causing market price to move up towards its guaranteed level. In healthy years, when demand is buoyant and when market price is well above the guaranteed level, De Beers will release diamonds from the stockpile allowing the price to float downwards to its guaranteed level. The CSO is therefore a buffer stock manager controlling market prices for uncut diamonds.

Success of the cartel depends very much on De Beers setting the guaranteed price more or less in line with the average natural equilibrium price – otherwise the organisation would be permanently stockpiling or selling from store uncut diamonds. It also requires the cartel members to abide by the rules and sell through the CSO rather than strike out independently; this Russia has obviously done from time to time.

**b** Russia independently sold uncut diamonds to the west and by so doing managed to earn $1 billion over an 18-month period. Earning foreign currency is vitally important for Russia as it struggles to come to terms with the market economy and a tremendous influx of foreign products. Russia clearly felt that the CSO had set the guaranteed price too low and that more was to be gained by allowing market forces to rule. However, it should be pointed out that if all diamond producers were to act independently and flood the market with diamonds the equilibrium price would fall substantially. Russia was, in fact, benefiting from the CSO's deliberate control of market supply.

Russia was also upset that the CSO did not take into account the opinions of its members in setting the guaranteed price for diamonds in the first place.

**c** If other countries found large qualities of uncut diamonds which were profitable to mine then the future of the CSO in controlling market prices would be much weakened **unless** the other countries joined the cartel. The strength of a cartel rests on creating a virtual monopoly seller of a product and if other countries refuse to join the Organisation its days are numbered. Already there is evidence of the cartel breaking up through the greed of one member – Russia – and on top of this, the data suggests that the CSO does not have a 100% cartel in uncut diamonds anyway.

**d** The price of a product is related to the marginal utility or satisfaction which it yields to the buyer rather than the total utility. In the case of diamonds, their shortage (which we have already seen may be deliberate) causes their marginal utility to be high – one diamond gives a lot of satisfaction to its owner – hence its market valuation (its price) is high. Conversely, water, although very essential and yielding a high total satisfaction, is in such plentiful supply in the UK, that the marginal satisfaction of one extra litre is very low. Thus, the price of water is relatively low in this country. Of course in countries where water is in shortage, it may be that the price of water is on par with the price of diamonds.

# Answers

## Data 19: Balance of payments accounting

**a** People in the UK do business with people overseas all through the year. They buy and sell goods and services; they make and receive investments on which income is earned; and they transfer funds in other ways. The balance of payments of each country records these monetary transactions between one country and the rest of the world. Structurally, the balance of payments is divided into the current account and the capital account. The current account records visible trade in goods between the UK and the rest of the world and invisible trade in services such as tourism and finance. In addition, the current account records investment income through, for example, international share dealing, and transfers the UK's government's contribution to the European Union.

**b** From the data provided in the diagram on page 37 it can be deduced that over the period 1970–94 the current account of the balance of payments has swung between deficits and surpluses. In all cases, the maximum deficit has always been greater than the maximum surplus. The most likely trend for the mid-1990s is a small surplus.

**c** In an accountancy sense the balance of payments will always balance. The current account records international flows of money paid for goods and services, earnings on investments and transfers. If the current account is in deficit, then the UK must be paying out more than it receives and this can only be undertaken by running down the UK's assets or increasing the UK's liabilities to other countries. A good analogy is a person who spends more than he or she earns. This can only be done by selling his or her assets (such as house or car), depleting financial assets or by borrowing from another source (increasing his or her liabilities). These transactions in assets and liabilities are recorded on the capital account of the balance of payments.

Theoretically, for every current account transaction there will be an equal and opposite capital account transaction. All exports are matched by an addition to the UK's net external assets and all imports are matched by a reduction in the UK's net external assets. Therefore, when people say that the UK has a *deficit* on the balance of payments they are, in fact, referring to the deficit on the current account. The capital account should show an equivalent surplus, so that the overall balance of payments is always in balance.

Finally, mention should be made of the 'balancing item' which is a statistical inclusion on the capital account to make up for any errors and omissions which might have taken place in the recording of these complicated money flows.

**d i** If the current account is in a fundamental deficit situation then high interest rates might be an attractive policy for the government. The high interest rates will attract into the country 'hot' money chasing the attractive returns on sterling. This in itself will begin to turn the deficit. In addition, the high interest rates will choke off consumer and producer expenditure not only for domestic goods and services, but also for imports. This, again, will help to reduce the deficit.

**ii** If sterling depreciates on the foreign exchange market then it is possible for the current account deficit to be turned. As sterling depreciates so the price of imports increase whilst our exports become more competitively priced. Hopefully, domestic consumers will reduce their demand for imports whilst foreigners increase their demand for exports. Obviously, the success of this policy will depend critically upon the value of the price elasticity of demand for both imports and exports. To be successful, the elasticity co-efficient must be greater than –1.

## Data 20: The UK's balance of trade regarding countries outside the EU

a The trade deficit, in this case, refers to the (negative) difference between our visible exports of goods and our visible imports of goods with non-EU countries. The data given suggests that in July of 1995 we imported £872 million worth of visible imports more than we exported and in August the trade deficit actually rose to £996 million.

b A devaluation of a currency means that the value of that currency is falling against other currencies. In 1992, the value of the pound significantly devalued on the foreign exchange market following the government's decision to remove sterling from the fixed exchange rate regime known as the ERM – the exchange rate mechanism. As the value of sterling fell, so in real terms the price of imports rose whilst in relation the price of UK exports fell. Higher import prices should result in falling demand for those goods and services, whilst cheaper exports should stimulate new markets for our goods and services. In effect, the trade deficit should reduce and might even turn into a surplus. However, a cautionary note – the effect of the change in import and export prices is very much determined by the price elasticity of demand for imports and exports. If demand for imports and exports is price inelastic then we can expect no overall improvement in our trading position following devaluation of the currency.

c Investment refers to the acquisition of capital goods such as tools, equipment and machinery which are vitally important for future growth of the economy. It is suggested in the data that the extra investment witnessed in the UK in 1995 is the result of importing these capital items rather than being able to produce them in the domestic economy.

d Investment is regarded as a direct injection into the circular flow of income (as is government expenditure on goods and services and exports). Being an injection, investment seeks to increase the national income resulting in extra production and employment which feeds through into standards of living of the community. An increase in investment of say £10 million does not automatically result in an increase of £10 million in national income since there is likely to a multiplier factor at work. In practice, the increase in investment on new machinery and equipment will initially be channelled into revenue of companies supplying the capital items who in turn will allocate the £10 million to the various resources which have been employed by the company. The recipients of this £10 million will in turn spend the vast majority of this sum – although some of it will be taxed, some will be saved and some will be spent on imported goods and services – thereby creating the income for a second generation of recipients. These, in turn, will spend the majority on domestically produced goods and services therefore creating income for another generation of recipients.

In this manner, from the initial investment of £10 million, a great deal more is being created and this will continue until national income rises sufficiently so as to equate injections with withdrawals from the circular flow of savings, imports and taxation.

e *Economic growth* occurs when the economy experiences an increase in output of goods and services which is associated with an increase in potential production. In terms of a production possibility curve (PPC), economic growth is reflected in the movement from any position on a PPC to a new position on another PPC which is further away from the origin. Thus the economy maintains maximum

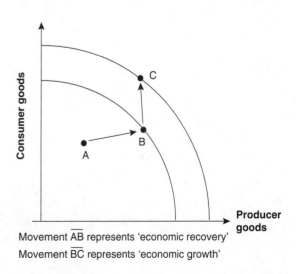

Movement $\overline{AB}$ represents 'economic recovery'

Movement $\overline{BC}$ represents 'economic growth'

production efficiency, but productive potential has increased. Investment in the form of new technology, increased equipment and tools, increases the productive capacity of the economy and therefore generates the economic growth described above.

*Economic recovery* occurs when the economy moves from within a PPC to a position onto a PPC. Thus the economy moves from an inefficient situation where there is either unemployment or a poor allocation of resources to a position on the PPC which indicates both full employment and full efficiency. The diagram at the bottom of page 59 illustrates both economic recovery and economic growth.

# Answers

## Data 21: The savings ratio

**a** Personal disposable income (PDI) refers to household or individual income which is available for expenditure. Therefore PDI is total income received from earnings (wages, interest, rent and profit) *plus* any state benefits such as child benefit, *plus* any private sources of income such as pension plans, but *less* income tax and national insurance.

**b** The information provided in the data refers to the savings ratio – the volume of savings as a percentage of real personal disposable income. The question asks whether personal savings are a direct function of personal disposable income and this can only be answered by calculating the volume of actual savings at various levels of income as follows:

| Year | Real PDI (£m) | Savings* (£m) |
|------|---------------|---------------|
| 1983 | 289,000 | 28,000 |
| 1984 | 300,000 | 33,300 |
| 1985 | 310,000 | 33,100 |
| 1986 | 324,000 | 28,100 |
| 1987 | 335,000 | 23,700 |
| 1988 | 355,000 | 20,200 |
| 1989 | 372,000 | 26,700 |
| 1990 | 379,000 | 31,800 |
| 1991 | 380,000 | 39,900 |
| 1992 | 390,000 | 49,900 |
| 1993 | 397,000 | 48,400 |

**Note:** *figures are rounded.

From this information we can now see that the relationship between PDI and savings is not always a direct one. For instance, between 1984 and 1988 PDI increased but savings decreased over the period. There are periods when both PDI and savings increased directly with each other, for example, between 1990 and 1992. In conclusion, the data does not provide sufficient evidence to state that there is a direct relationship between the two variables of PDI and savings.

**c** From the answer above, there would seem to be other factors in the economy influencing the volume of savings apart from the level of PDI. Certainly interest rates must play an important role in determining savings decisions. When interest rates are high the attraction to save is greater and vice versa.

The age composition of the household is important too. Young people typically have high propensities to spend and low propensities to save. With age comes the desire and the wherewithal to save, which in later years is turned back round again to generate consumption.

The effect of inflation on savings is unclear. On the one hand, it is possible that as households and individuals begin to fear inflation they may prefer to bring forward their consumption and as a result the volume of savings diminishes. On the other hand, the erosion of the real value of savings during inflationary periods may persuade households and individuals to increase their savings in an attempt to restore their real value.

Certainly expectation plays a role in determining the volume of savings. If the economic outlook is gloomy and jobs are felt to be insecure then individuals may respond by reducing their expenditure and saving more for the future. The 'feel-good' factor is certainly important when it comes to savings decisions.

The distribution of the nation's income is also considered important. Those on high incomes typically have high marginal propensities to save whilst those on lower incomes have a much lower propensity to save. Therefore government polices designed to redistribute income towards the lower income groups are usually accompanied by upward shifts in the consumption function and, conversely, downward shifts in the savings function.

**d** A fall in personal savings can have a negative effect on the volume of investment in the economy. A great deal of investment in the private sector is undertaken through borrowed funds from specialist institutions and from commercial banks. If savings levels are falling there will be insufficient funds available for private industry, investment in capital equipment will diminish and this, in turn, will affect economic growth.

A second effect of reduced savings propensities is that this must imply that consumption levels are rising. The economy must be increasing its expenditure levels – aggregate demand is rising. Unless supply can increase proportionately, there will be pressure on the price level to rise.

If personal savings are falling this must imply that personal consumption is rising. If the extra consumption is on domestic goods then we can expect to enjoy a fall in the level of recorded unemployment. However, if the extra consumption is in the form of increased imports, then the effect of the decrease in personal savings is possibly to move the economy into a balance of trade deficit.

## Data 22: Measuring inflation

**a** As a first step, it is important to realise that in the calculation of the average rate of inflation consideration must be taken of the relative 'weights' associated with each of the commodities in the 'basket'. In this particular case, for example, the price of food has risen by 10% and it takes up a considerable proportion of consumer's expenditure, –40%. Therefore the contribution of food to the overall rate of inflation must be significant. Contrast this with household durables. Although the price of these items have also gone up by 10% they only account for a meagre 5% of consumer expenditure and so the contribution of household durables to the overall rate of inflation must be quite low.

Calculation of the rate of inflation should proceed as shown in the table below.

**b** From the information above, the average rate of inflation in Utopia is 4.35%. However, this inflation rate is based on the *average* price change of *selected* commodities undertaken by the *average* consumer and both the Smiths and the Forsyths might not be the 'average' couple. Therefore the average rate of inflation calculated in this manner cannot be a perfect indicator of either couple's personal inflation rate.

For example, the Smiths tend to shop locally and since they live in a rural area where local shops tend to have higher than usual prices it might well be that the rate of inflation personally to this couple is somewhat higher than that calculated. This might be made worse by the fact that they tend to spend a very large proportion of their income on food, even more than 40%, which given its significant price rise over the period will result in a personal inflation rate which is higher than the average of 4.35%.

Although the increased price of energy might benefit the Smiths, who tend to stay in rather more than the Forsyths, this might be offset by the benefit which the latter couple is receiving in terms of lower petrol costs compared to the former who do not possess a car. Indeed, the Smiths tend to rely on public transport and there has been no price reduction for this elderly couple in this area. One would have to question seriously the relevance of the selected commodities and the percentage of consumer expenditure spent on these commodities for both couples.

It is unlikely that the Smiths would spend as high a percentage of their income on housing as the younger couple, nor on entertainment, and this results in the average inflation rate being an imperfect indicator of the rate of inflation to both couples.

A further consideration is the fact that the Smiths receive a fixed income in the form of an occupational and a state pension. Inflation erodes much more severely into fixed incomes

| Commodity | Percentage average price change | Percentage of consumer expenditure spent on average | Weighting | Weighting × price change |
|---|---|---|---|---|
| Food | +10 | 40 | 40 | +400 |
| Transport | 0 | 10 | 10 | 0 |
| Entertainment | +5 | 5 | 5 | +25 |
| Energy/fuel | –5 | 15 | 15 | –75 |
| Housing | +2 | 20 | 20 | +40 |
| Household durables | +10 | 5 | 5 | +50 |
| Other | –1 | 5 | 5 | –5 |
| **Totals** | | | **100** | **435** |

So the average rate of inflation in Utopia is given by: 435 ÷ 100 = 4.35%

compared to incomes such as that received by the Forsyths who are more likely to see their earnings keep up with the rate of inflation. The Forsyths also have their savings invested in equity shares and the dividends on these shares are reflected in the profit made by the companies. As such, dividends will tend to rise, although not perfectly, in line with the rate of inflation.

Examining the situation rather more closely for the Forsyths we have to note that the commodity categories might need widening and their weightings altered to give a better picture of the rate of inflation effect on this couple. Assuming that foreign holidays, for example, are included in the commodity 'other' it might be more plausible to increase the percentage of income spent on this area and perhaps reduce the percentage of income spent on food and public transport. Finally, it should be noted that the younger couple might be adversely affected by living in the capital city of Utopia where prices tend to be higher, in general, than in other regions.

Obviously, without accurate information on which commodities the two couples actually purchase and the percentage of their income spent on these commodities it is impossible to arrive at a conclusion as to whether the calculated rate of inflation accurately reflects their personal rates. However, the information presented tends to imply that the Smiths are more adversely affected personally by inflation than the Forsyths.

# Answers

## Data 23: Tories plan U-turn on car culture

**a** There are several reasons why the government may reduce the current road building programme. In the first instance, there has been a lot of opposition from environmentalists concerning the physical effects of road building on wild life and natural resources, and the effect of an ever-increasing use of the car and other vehicles on the community. The problem is that road usage has noted adverse externalities in the form of increased risk of accidents, congestion and pollution. The data points to a possible link between road use and asthma, and there is also reference to rising traffic levels 'stifling' cities and towns.

Another reason why the government might be considering a reduction in the road building programme is that this will allow it to reduce its public spending and therefore its public spending borrowing requirement (PSBR).

**b** **Note:** There are several relevant policies which could be described and explained and full marks should be awarded to any two which are technically accurate and which are developed in depth.

One policy is to increase the excise tax on petrol – the data suggests a possibility of a further rise of 13p. Consider the diagram below left which shows the possible effect of a tax placed on petrol.

Without the tax the number of litres of petrol bought and sold is $X_1$ and the price of a litre of petrol is $Y_1$. The problem is that the supply curve of petrol as given by $S_1$ reflects only the private costs of petrol consumption. The full social costs of petrol consumption are given by the supply curve $S_2$. This is a reflection of both private costs and the adverse externalities that petrol consumption brings – pollution, congestion and so on. The government uses a tax of T to force $S_1$ to $S_2$ causing the final equilibrium price of petrol to rise to $Y_2$ and the amount of petrol bought and sold to fall to $X_2$. Since less petrol is now bought and sold, there will be less adverse externalities imposed on the community.

Notice that the price of petrol to the consumer has not increased by the full amount of the tax – there is a shared burden between the producer and the consumer.

A second policy which the government could introduce is to subsidise public transport to such an extent that the community is tempted to use buses and trains in preference to private transport. The cost of the subsidy will be born by the taxpayer. Diagrammatically we have the situation in the figure below right.

The original price for the bus service is given by $Y_1$ and $X_1$ passengers are tempted to use the service at this price. A subsidy of S will cause the supply of bus services to shift to $S_2$ causing a new equilibrium at $Y_2$ and $X_2$. More passengers now prefer to take public transport thereby reducing the pressure on roads. Apart from the subsidy which will, in this case, be shared between producers and passengers, the government should also look towards improving the quality of the service for public

Price | Numbers of litres

MSC = Marginal social cost
MPC = Marginal private cost
T = tax

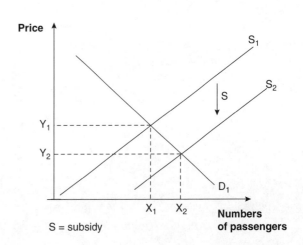

S = subsidy

Price | Numbers of passengers

65

transport if it is to really attract passengers from private vehicle use.

Another possible policy which might be used to persuade car owners to use public transport is a system of road pricing. There are many possible alternatives including fitting cars with some form of meter which can either be fed with pre-paid cards or with an annual meter reading which is followed by a bill. Motorways are likely to be initially targeted and it is a possibility that the meters will be activated by beacons set alongside the carriageway. The beacons can then be programmed to charge more as congestion rates reach their peak levels. Obviously the cost of implementing such a system would be very expensive and there would be considerable running costs. In addition, politically the move towards road pricing in this manner might be very damaging as motorists, rightly or wrongly, perceive roads as a 'free' good.

One further alternative to consider is increasing the provision of new roads and improving existing roads. Many organisations are in favour of improving our road stock – and many of these organisations (e.g. the AA, RAC and the British Road Federation) have an interest in maintaining the supremacy of the private car. Bypass schemes and motorways take traffic away from congested areas and so reduce pollution as well as reducing journey times. However, environmentalists would argue that further adverse externalities are created as the countryside is eaten into by the car economy.

c   The success of the licensing system will depend very much on the price elasticity of demand for private motoring. Most motorists have quite inelastic demand for car usage – even when the cost of petrol, insurance or maintenance goes up quite substantially, private vehicles will still be used. The cost of the licences would therefore have to be fairly large for motorists to consider car sharing or using public transport. To aid success the government might consider some form of marketing to encourage motorists to leave their cars at home.

# Answers

## Data 24: Minister condemns EU over tobacco farm aid

**a** The British government's main policy towards stopping smoking is through indirect taxation. Tax on cigarettes in Britain is currently £2.11 (per packet of 20) – the fourth highest within the EU. The greater the price elasticity of demand for cigarettes, the more successful higher levels of indirect tax on cigarettes will be in persuading consumers to stop smoking. Therefore, if the demand for cigarettes is price inelastic, and after all cigarettes are addictive, then there will be a check on the success of taxation as an anti-smoking policy.

Another useful policy undertaken by the British government in its anti-smoking campaign is restrictive tobacco advertising and promotions. Tobacco products cannot be advertised on TV and must be limited in any media form which is attractive to young people. Tobacco products, too, must carry a warning of the inherent health dangers. There does seem to be a constraint on the success of this policy – the industry seems to come up with novel advertising ideas which are outside the restrictions – sponsorship of sporting events is very prominent within the industry.

**b** An efficient allocation of scarce resources occurs when the price consumers pay is equal to the marginal costs of production. This would indicate that consumers neither want more nor less of the product. Smoking represents a misallocation of resources because smoking imposes adverse externalities upon the community – the detrimental effects of passive smoking are well documented. Consider the diagram below left.

Given that the demand curve reflects consumers' valuation of the product and MPC represents the marginal private costs of cigarette production – the supply curve – the free market would give rise to market equilibrium of $P_1$ and $Q_1$. The consumption of the cigarettes will impose adverse externalities onto the community.

MSC represents the marginal social costs of cigarette production. It is the aggregate of the MPC plus the adverse externalities. So long as the government can force producers to cover their marginal social costs, usually through indirect taxation (t), the market equilibrium will settle at $P_2$ and $Q_2$. Notice that there will be fewer cigarettes smoked and hence the adverse externalities are diminished.

**c** European tobacco farmers are subsidised through the farm support system of the Common Agricultural Policy of the EU. (The European Community developed into the European Union with the advent of more member countries.) Consider the diagram below right.

The natural equilibrium price for tobacco is given by $P_1$, but the CAP system chooses to impose a guaranteed price of $P_G$ onto the market. At this price, demand falls, whilst supply increases, and the CAP is forced to purchase the excess supply of tobacco from the

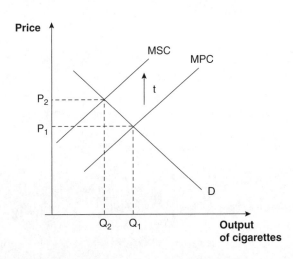

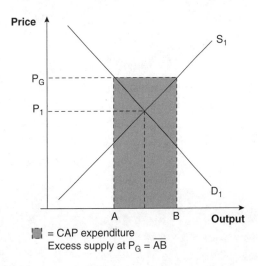

= CAP expenditure
Excess supply at $P_G = \overline{AB}$

market in order to maintain $P_G$. The expenditure undertaken by CAP is estimated to be £3 million a day and is shown by the shaded area on the diagram.

Tobacco, like many other farm products cannot be stored by CAP indefinitely. If the tobacco is released back into the European market, tobacco prices would fall towards their natural equilibrium level – much to the detriment of the farmers. In order to avoid wastage, CAP is likely to sell the tobacco off cheaply to Third World countries.

# Answers

## Data 25: Government finances

**a** Government borrowing from the private sector may well crowd out private sector investment and ultimately affect the rate of economic growth. If the government is borrowing from us, there will be less money available for us to channel into industry either directly through share ownership or indirectly through the banking institutions. Even where finance is available industry will find that its price – the rate of interest to be paid on loans – will be unusually high and therefore the demand for borrowed money for investment purposes will diminish. Since investment is an important prerequisite for economic growth and allows the economy's production possibility curve to be pushed outwards, the effects on future growth are detrimental.

**b i** Interest rates influence the level of employment in the economy by their effect on both consumer and producer expenditure. When interest rates are low, both these forms of expenditure will tend to increase since consumption and investment are both largely undertaken by borrowed finance. If the cost of credit is low the volume of expenditure is high and this will have a positive effect on the level of employment, and vice versa.

**ii** Interest rates also play a role in determining the value of the exchange rate. High rates of interest will attract 'hot' money into the economy looking for the highest return. Thus the demand for that currency, in this case sterling, will rise and so will the value of the currency. This is shown in the following diagram.

Originally, the value of sterling is such that £1 = $2, where demand and supply

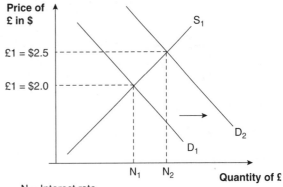

N = Interest rate
D = Demand
D = Supply

for the currency are equal. High interest rates in the UK cause the demand for sterling to rise and thus the value of the dollar will appreciate to its new equilibrium level where £1 = $2.5.

**c** The true cost to the economy of continual government borrowing is first the effect of higher rates of interest on the economy. In order to borrow more and more the government must attract funds and that means bidding up the rate of interest in the economy. This can have negative effects on the level of unemployment as described earlier. In addition, the higher rates of interest will cause the interest repayments on the national debt to increase significantly. In the data it is suggesting that interest repayments on the national debt cost the economy almost as much as the National Health Service.

**d** A balanced budget occurs when the revenue into the Exchequer – taxation and borrowing – is equal to government expenditure on goods and services in the economy. Even a balanced budget, however, will have an expansionary force upon the level of national income.

# SECTION C: EXAMINATION PRACTICE

# The M&S of water – a step ahead of demand

THE PHILOSOPHY of Marks & Spencer looms large in the thinking of the man who is a keen player in the profits growth of Welsh Water plc.

'M&S has 80% of the market in men's underwear, which is virtually a monopoly, but is constantly improving the product', said Graham Hawker the Chief Executive of Welsh Water. 'We have to be the Marks & Spencer of the water industry, which means being one step ahead of customer aspirations all of the time.'

In looking at the company's achievements since privatisation he believes the regulatory businesses of water and sewerage are becoming more efficient. But he acknowledges that while the

company was attempting to satisfy the tough 'clean-up standards' set by the National Rivers Authority customers were becoming disenchanted with the costs involved which were hitting their pockets through soaring bills.

'We went to the customers and asked their views, and although we were warned that we would get a 2% response the figure turned out to be 15%. Clearly consumers wanted a chance to put across their views. From next April the increase in charges to consumers will be 0.5% above inflation, and we have only been able to achieve this by becoming more efficient over the last five years. Forecasts originally indicated that the

increase would be 5.5% above inflation.'

Graham Hawker believes that there must be a fair balance between customer needs and shareholders' expectations. 'If we don't look after the customers then the shareholders will pay the price in the end', he said. 'Welsh water is leading the way in the industry on environmental cleaning-up and that is good for shareholders.'

Welsh Water's workforce pre-privatisation totalled around 4000 but the figure is now down to around 3000 and is likely to come down even further in the pursuit of greater efficiency and cost-effectiveness.

(Adapted from the *Western Mail*, November 1994)

**Note:** The data provided here and the consequent questions were written prior to SWALEC's take-over of Welsh Water, and the creation of the Environment Agency to take over functions previously carried out by the National Rivers Authority in 1996.

## Questions

**a** The Chief Executive for Welsh Water plc seems to be suggesting that some *monopolies* do not constantly improve their products for the benefit of their customers – unlike M&S. What features concerning monopolies might allow them to treat their customers in such a disparaging manner? **(4)**

**b** Welsh Water, in the past, has been accused of polluting the river ways, which the Environment Agency is now putting right by forcing the industry to 'clean up'. This has had the ultimate effect of forcing up consumer charges for water and

sewerage treatment. Using *economic principles* explain this
argument.                                                          **(12)**

**c** How do you think that Welsh Water has become more 'efficient
... since privatisation'?                                          **(5)**

**d** Explain why the Chief Executive for Welsh Water believes that
if customers are not well looked after 'shareholders will pay the
price in the end'.                                                 **(4)**

---

# Student guide

### THE M&S OF WATER – A STEP AHEAD

**1** The title is not very informative – you should move on quickly to
a careful reading of the article.

**2** As you undertake your reading, make quick summaries in the margin
and/or jot down any relevant economic theory which comes to mind.
For example:

| Paragraph 2 | M&S referred to as a 'monopoly' in men's underwear, but quality still important. |
| Paragraph 3 | Privatisation of water utility – regulatory body, OFWAT, dealing with adverse externalities. |
| Paragraph 4 | Dealing with adverse externalities means charging customers more but charges are not as much as thought – EFFICIENCY. |
| Paragraph 5 | Customers' and shareholders' interests differ – why? |
| Paragraph 6 | Privatisation and job losses. |

**3** Check the mark weightings for the questions. Don't waste valuable
time on questions which carry few marks.

**4** Mix the data provided with your own economic theory – never one
or the other.

**5** Do not get persuaded into giving a political argument. You are a
*positive* economist for rather than a *normative* economist.

**6** However, some economic history perspective might benefit your
answer.

# The effective exchange rate

Examine the following data:

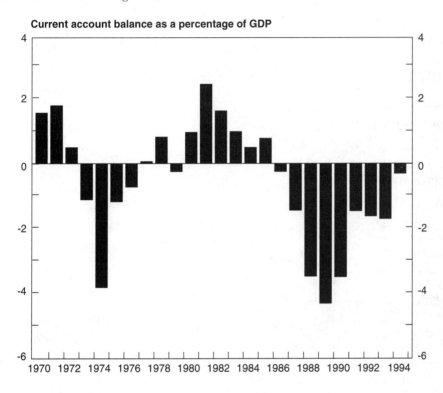

**Current account balance as a percentage of GDP**

Source: CSO

*Current account balance*

| Sterling effective exchange rate (1985 = 100) | |
|---|---|
| 1975 | 124.8 |
| 1977 | 101.2 |
| 1979 | 107.0 |
| 1981 | 119.0 |
| 1983 | 105.3 |
| 1985 | 100.0 |
| 1987 | 90.1 |
| 1989 | 92.6 |
| 1991 | 91.7 |
| 1993 | 80.2 |

Source: *Economic Trends 1995*, HMSO

| Selected retail banks: short-term money rates | |
|---|---|
| 1975 | 10.0% |
| 1977 | 8.0% |
| 1979 | 14.0% |
| 1981 | 14.0% |
| 1983 | 9.5% |
| 1985 | 11.5% |
| 1987 | 10.0% |
| 1989 | 15.0% |
| 1991 | 11.0% |

Source: *Economic Trends 1995*, HMSO

## Questions

**a** How would you explain the difference between the 'effective exchange rate' and a *single currency exchange rate*? **(5)**

**b** What relationship would you expect between the *balance of payments on current account* and the 'effective exchange rate'? Does the data provided match your expectations? **(10)**

**c** What information would you wish to examine in making a judgement about the cause of changes in the effective exchange rate? **(10)**

# Student guide

## THE EFFECTIVE EXCHANGE RATE

1  When presented with statistical data of this nature you really need to sit back and decide exactly what information is being presented to you! You cannot answer this question unless you have a precise understanding of both 'the effective exchange rate' and 'the current account balance'.

   The *effective exchange rate* is an index which measures the value of one currency (sterling) against a basket of other currencies to give an average valuation of the one currency.

   The *current account balance* is one section of the overall balance of payments and it records monetary movements between the UK and the rest of the world for trade in visible goods, invisible services, investments and monetary transfers.

2  Make sure you read the headings, labels and titles of the tables and graph very carefully. 1985 is the base year and has an index value of 100 – the effective exchange rate measures the changes in the value of the currency against this base year. The vertical axis of the graph measures the current account balance as a percentage of GDP. What is most significant is a recognition that when the 'bars' dip below 0, this implies the UK has a deficit on the current account.

3  Try to look for connections between the two sets of data. Are there years when the effective exchange rate is falling and the current account soon moves into surplus? Would you expect this?

4  Look carefully at the questions, and of course the mark weightings. Don't forget to extract data trends to support your answer.

# The Utopian economy

The following information refers to Utopia which is a small economy and which does not involve itself with international trade.

Household consumption on goods and services in Utopia is given by the equation:

$$C = 2,000 + 0.8 \, Y_d$$

where C is consumption and $Y_d$ is disposable income.

The Utopian government raises all of its revenue by means of a direct tax on income and the tax rate is a flat or proportional rate of 25% of income. This can be expressed as:

$$T = 0.25 Y_t$$

where T is the tax revenue and $Y_t$ is the total income.

Private investment by Utopian companies is £800 and government spending on goods and services is £3,200.

**Note:** all figures are in £ billions.

## Questions

a  Comment on the nature of the household consumption function
   using a diagram to illustrate your answer.                              **(7)**
b  What is the level of equilibrium national income in the Utopian
   economy?                                                                **(6)**
c  Assume that unemployment exists in Utopia and that the
   government appreciates that it needs to create £1,000 billion to
   eliminate unemployment. How much extra spending should the
   government undertake on goods and services to do this?                  **(7)**
d  What is the change in the budgetary position for the government
   comparing the new equilibrium level of income with the old
   equilibrium level of income?                                           **(5)**

# Student guide

**THE UTOPIAN ECONOMY**

1 Unfortunately, there is not much guidance which can be offered with these type of questions. There are two main problems which might arise if you choose to complete one of these, assuming there is a choice in an examination:

* your maths might let you down
* very often your success in answering the latter parts of the question is dependent upon your answer in the earlier parts. This means that you could score very good marks or very low marks.

2 To assist you in this question you might like to consider the following points:

*Disposable income* This is the income which is available for spending. In this case it is total income less taxation

*The consumption function* This is given in terms of disposable income, but you will need to convert that into terms of total income.
Remember that taxes are 0.25 of $Y_t$ so therefore disposable income is 0.75 of $Y_t$.

*Equilibrium income* Either use the withdrawals = injections approach, $S + T = I + G$ or remember that $Y = C + I + G$.
Remember, this is a closed economy!

*The multiplier* $1/(MPS + MPT)$

*Budgetary position* You will need to calculate the difference between government expenditure and taxation revenue.

3 Unless you are very confident with these sorts of questions and have had practice in them, you are advised to steer clear of these during examinations!

# Bankers declare war on the currency dealers

AUGUST IS A MONTH for starting wars as well as ending them. Central bankers appear to have joined the generals of the First World War in choosing it as the month for the start of hostilities. Their targets are the dealers who pushed the yen and the mark to such dizzy heights earlier this year. In a triple alliance between the Japanese, American and German central banks, helped by supporting fire from the Swiss National Bank, there was no doubt who is winning the day. The dollar broke through what had been seen as a critical technical support level of about Y94.60 and then advanced a further Y2 in hectic trading yesterday.

The question now is just how far the dollar rally has to go. Already it has gained more than most currency strategists were predicting for weeks, if not months to come. The market now has Y100 and DM1.50 in its sights, but there must be considerable doubt over whether the rally can be sustained much beyond those levels.

As we were reminded by a paper published by the Bank of England two weeks ago, foreign exchange markets are more often than not dominated by "epidemics or herd behaviour". Dealers watch what others are doing and copy them if they are successful. It is this feature that the central banks have exploited so successfully in their recent tactics. There are no dealers watched more closely than central banks. Well publicised intervention has clearly convinced traders that there is a lot of money to be lost by betting against the dollar. Dollar weakness has generally been attributed to the US twin budgetary and balance of payments deficits, which have led to a continuous outflow of dollars for so many years. Yen strength has equally been attributed to the Japanese tendency to over-save and to pile up huge surpluses.

In the next year or so, the current account trends look favourable. One of the factors that helped the dollar to strengthen yesterday against the yen was the marked reduction in the Japanese trade balance in July. It had been falling for some time in yen, but because of the appreciation of the yen had been slower to come down in dollar terms. Equally, the US trade deficit is generally expected to fall quite substantially in the months ahead.

The budgetary trends are also more favourable to the US than is generally acknowledged. The US budget deficit is now less than 2 per cent of GDP. There appears to be a real willingness to tackle the deficits that have dogged US public finances since President Reagan cut taxes without commensurate reductions in spending.

Source: The *Independent*, August 1995

## Questions

**a** Assuming floating exchange rates, explain how dealers have managed to push the yen and the mark 'to such dizzy heights earlier this year'. (5)

**b** How do you suppose the triple alliance between the Japanese, American and German central banks has succeeded in pushing up the value of the dollar? (5)

**c** What does the Bank of England mean when it states that foreign exchange markets are more often than not dominated by 'epidemics or herd behaviour'? (5)

**d** Explain why the dollar has largely been a weak currency over the last decade or more. What underlying features are there now in the American economy to suggest that the dollar might recover in the future? (10)

# Student guide

### BANKERS DECLARE WAR ON THE CURRENCY DEALERS

**1** This is quite a revealing headline. What do currency dealers do? *Buy and sell currency* **to** make profit. What happens to international exchange rates as a result? *They become unstable.* So how can the banks stop this instability? *They can act together to buy or sell in opposition.*

**2** Read through the newspaper article carefully, jotting down relevant economic theory or summary points, where appropriate. For example:

| Paragraph 1 | Dealers in the past had forced up yen and franc, now the Japanese, French and US banks forcing up the dollar. |
|---|---|
| Paragraph 3 | Bank of England refers to the dealers working in herds – following each other. The bank alliance has persuaded the dealers that they mean business in pushing the dollar up – dealers now want the dollar. Why was the dollar low? Balance of payments and budget. |
| Paragraph 4 | US economy is looking good – will the dollar keep going up? |
| Paragraph 5 | As above. |

**3** Check the mark weighting for each question – do not waste time on questions which carry few marks.

**4** Read questions carefully and mix data with relevant economic theory.

**5** Can you include any relevant diagrams which will assist your explanation? If you do the diagrams must be accurate, well labelled and referred to in your written answer.

# Dairy farms go down the drain

**Michael Durham**

## New quota chaos milked by speculators

Every morning, farmer Brian Nicholas carefully collects 800 litres of milk – fresh, creamy and frothing – and then tips it all into his muck spreader.

The milk, from his herd of 80 Jersey cows, is sprayed like liquid fertiliser over the fields on his farm in north Devon.

Mr Nicholas, a small dairy farmer, is one of hundreds of producers forced by European Union milk quotas to throw away his produce this year, following deregulation of the milk industry in November.

The result could be a milk drought next month, as production slows down. Yet, as some farmers are going out of business, others – land-owners, middle-men and even some country-dwellers who have never raised a cow – are making large sums by trading in EU milk quotas, which are alleged to be the cause of all the trouble.

The crisis in the industry, widely predicted when the Milk Marketing Board was replaced in November with Milk Marque and a handful of other deregulated dairy businesses, looks like coming to a head.

Although analysts say a milk shortage is unlikely to affect shop prices – because milk will be diverted from cheese and yoghurt manufacture to fill pint bottles – the long-term consequences for Britain's dairy industry could be enormous.

This winter is the worst on record for small dairy farmers. The quota system, introduced 10 years ago, is supposed to limit British milk production by setting a ceiling on each farmer's productivity. But a sudden rise in quota prices has upset the market.

For Brian and Diane Nicholas, who farm 120 acres at Woodhouse Farm, South Molton, Devon, the combination of a mild autumn and rising quota prices has been disastrous. They own 150,000 litres of quota, although the farm actually produces 300,000 litres each year. They normally bridge the gap between their official limit by leasing quota from other farmers at around 6p per litre.

This year, since deregulation, the cost of the quotas has risen fivefold, peaking at more than 30p per litre. The best price a farmer can hope to get for his milk is about 23p to 24p a litre.

To make matters worse, a mild autumn meant cattle kept producing large amounts of milk. 'We ran out of our own quota early on,' said Mrs Nicholas. 'It's uneconomic to lease any more. Since 1 January, we have been pouring our milk into the dung spreader.'

If farmers send more than their annual quota of milk to market, they are fined heavily. Unable to sell their milk, they nevertheless have to keep their cattle fed and their farms running smoothly.

Ashley Sutton, another Devon farmer, knows of 'hundreds of farmers who may go out of business in the next 12 months'.

With quota prices high, millions of litres of quota are being leased or sold, producing unexpected fortunes. The quota price took off with deregulation of the milk industry. Milk quota is tied to land, but not necessarily to dairy farms. Many retired farmers have hung on to quota as an investment to supplement their pensions, and now find they have a valuable nest-egg.

Many big landowners are also believed to own quota. The number of 'quota agents' – middle-men who match supply and demand of quotas in the milk industry – is believed to have doubled in the past 18 months.

There have even been rumours – firmly denied – of City speculation in milk quotas, and of sporting personalities and football clubs buying millions of pounds of quota as a form of investment.

To small farmers, the idea that non-milk producers can get rich while the farmers themselves pour away milk is scandalous. 'We view it as sheer corruption,' said Mrs Nicholas. 'Britain is the only country which allows quota leasing. It's against the whole spirit of the quota system.'

She is to visit lawyers this week to see if quota leasing can be challenged in the European Court.

As one independent expert observed, however, 'quotas were introduced to reduce milk production – and they have certainly been effective'. Those farmers forced to pour their milk on to the land will ruefully agree.

Source: The *Observer*, February 1995

a   Why did the European Community (the precursor to the
    European Union) impose milk quotas on farmers some ten
    years ago?                                                   **(10)**
b   Since the introduction of the quotas, farmers have been able to
    sell their unused quota to other farmers wanting to increase
    their production beyond their allocated limits. Why has the price
    of trade quotas risen sharply since 'deregulation' of the milk
    industry in the UK?                                          **(10)**
c   How far would you agree that milk quotas are an excellent
    form of investment?                                          **(5)**

# Student guide

### DAIRY FARMS GO DOWN THE DRAIN

1   This is an usually long newspaper extract and will take some careful
    reading! A highlighter pen might prove a useful tool!

2   Read the sub-title carefully – this gives you more information than
    the main title. What is a *quota*? A limit on production – in this case,
    milk.

3   Read each extract through now, highlighting relevant economic
    theory and making summary notes. For example:

| | |
|---|---|
| Column 1 Paragraph 3 | Supply of milk more than quota – throw away surplus – EU. |
| Paragraph 4 | Some farmers going bankrupt. There is a separate business in selling EU milk quotas. |
| Paragraph 5 | Deregulation in UK milk industry – more competition. |
| Paragraph 7 | Quota prices going up – bankruptcy for some farmers? |
| Column 2 Paragraph 1 | Shows how some farmers have to buy quotas from others to produce more milk than their own quotas allow. |
| Paragraph 2,3,4,5 | Refers to quota prices going up – farmers can't afford to buy quotas – pour milk away; bankruptcies. |
| Column 3 Paragraph 1 | Some farmers making a lot of money by selling their quotas on to those who want them – the speculators. |
| Paragraph 2,3 | Further examples of quota speculators. |

**4** Check the mark weightings for the questions – don't waste time on questions which carry too few marks to the detriment of other, more heavily weighted questions.

**5** Mix the data with the relevant theory – make sure you do not copy 'chunks' from the data!

**6** Diagrams are appropriate but should be well labelled, accurate and should be referred to in your written answer.

# Don't shoot the economist

ECONOMISTS undeniably have a bad name. Blamed for the economic ills of the nation – as if policy makers had nothing to do with policy or managers with business – economists are accused of inhabiting a fantasy world of their own unrealistic models and are unable to arrive at any consensus opinion to any question asked of them. What have they done to deserve this?

Getting into macroeconomic forecasting is maybe one thing. This is a chancy business, to be sure. But forecasting the economy is only one small aspect of the work of the economist. Economists do not spend most of their time on macroeconomics – they spend a large part of it on microeconomics, dealing with the behaviour of individual consumers, and producer and market behaviour.

Against the grand-sounding macroeconomics, microeconomics may sound rather puny, but from a study of micro decisions economists discover the factors affecting the performance of the economy as a whole. At this stage you enter the 'unrealistic' phase. The microeconomic model of perfect competition, held in so much esteem by economists, is not the world that real companies and real managers inhabit. Yet it is wrong to say that economists have taken up the model of perfect competition to describe the world *as it is*. As Professor Frank Hahn argued in Cambridge over 20 years ago, the model of perfect competition tackles the question 'What would the real world *have to be like* for de-centralised decision making by individual consumers and firms, co-ordinated only by market exchange and the working of the price mechanism, to lead to an *ideal state of society*?'

The answer is the model of perfect competition with all its 'unreal' assumptions. If this is unworldly, don't blame the economists for the fact that the real world does not come up to what is needed for markets 'to work'. Rather, qualify our faith in the market mechanism and change government policy accordingly.

But this is all heady stuff, far removed from what passes over the desk of most managers or through most consumers' minds at the point of sale in the local supermarket. Does economics have anything to offer at this level? The answer is most certainly 'yes'. How common is the knee-jerk response to an operating deficit to put up prices! Yet as any first-year economics student knows, if demand is price elastic, raising prices will result in a fall in revenue; better in this case to reduce prices.

Or consider the fundamental principle of opportunity cost. Businesses may have quite a good understanding of opportunity cost of their physical resources, but when capital investment decisions take into account the rate of interest which would have been earned on internally generated funds from elsewhere then thank the economist.

Or take the universally applicable economic decision rule of 'equating at the margin' – ensuring that the last £10 spent on food benefits the family just as much as the last £10 spent on the car; the last £1,000 spent on staff wages benefits the company just as much as the last £1,000 spent on new machinery. If not, then the utility of the family or the profits of the company can be increased by switching from one expenditure area into the other until the equalities hold.

Elasticity, opportunity cost and equating at the margin are all part of the fall-out of economists' inquiry into high level matters of resource allocation. These are the simple, practical truths of economics and there are many more.

(Adapted from an article by John Cable, *The Observer*, January 1995)

## Questions

a How far do you agree that the assumptions of the model of
perfect competition are 'unreal'? (8)

b If the world were to be characterised by perfect competition
why and how would there be an 'ideal state of society'? (7)

c Explain why price increases will result in lower revenues if
demand is price elastic. (5)

d Using relevant examples, explain one other economic concept
which has application to the 'real world'. (5)

# Student guide

**DON'T SHOOT THE ECONOMIST**

1 There is certainly not much to be gained from the headline, this
time!

2 Although this is quite a lengthy piece of prose, it is still advisable
to jot down any relevant theory and/or summary. For example:

| Paragraph 1 | Is economics unreal? |
|---|---|
| Paragraph 2 | Economists deal with micro and macro aspects. |
| Paragraph 3 | Perfect competition – is it unrealistic? Assumptions? Ideal state for society/resources? |
| Paragraph 5 | Real business world – economics does offer something (eg elasticity). |
| Paragraph 6 | Opportunity cost. |
| Paragraph 7 | Principle of substitution and equi-marginal principle. |

**Note:** the words/phrases in italics might be worth closer consideration.

3 As always, check the mark weightings to avoid wasting time on questions which carry few marks.

4 Notice, again, that the question itself is carrying phrases in italics.
Refer back to the text to help you gain understanding.

5 Diagrams will benefit your answer if they are accurate, well labelled
and are referred to in your written answer.

6 Remember to mix economic theory with information gleaned from
the data provided.

# Freedom to work is not a part-time principle

ONE TREND WE can be thankful for is the fall in the rate of growth of unemployment. But what is exactly happening in the labour market and why?

The Chancellor at the recent Labour Market Summit in Detroit spoke of *'deregulation and flexibility'*, but this didn't impress Robert Reich the US Labour Secretary. Reich is a great advocate of flexibility in the sense of improving the skills of the workforce and increasing the mobility of labour but after one look at the European contribution to the jobs summit, Reich said 'When you (Europe) hear the word flexibility, watch your wallets.' As he rightly diagnosed for the British government, flexibility means 'freedom to fire people and to reduce wages'.

Deregulation and flexibility were with us in the 1990–92 recession and did precious little to help the unemployed then. Even the recent reduction in the unemployment figures is more to do with the devaluation of the pound following our departure from the fixed exchange rate system of the ERM than anything to do with deregulation and flexibility.

Thankfully, there are also demographic trends at work which are tending to reduce the number of people out of work – as more people stay on at school after 16 and others take up early retirement offers.

The upturn in the economy, stimulated by devaluation of the pound and lower interest rates, has reduced the rate at which people are being declared redundant. However, there is little job creation to talk about – it is more a situation of a reduction in job destruction. Whereas 353,000 people moved onto the unemployment register in February 1993, some 28,000 fewer signed on this February.

There are still millions of people in the UK and continental Europe who want to work, but have neither a part-time nor a full-time job at present. A lot of them are well educated too. A good supply-side needs a good demand-side.

What Europe needs now is typically Keynesian style policies in favour of public expenditure.

(Adapted from an article by William Keegan, following the Labour Market Summit in Detroit, The *Observer*, March 1994)

## Questions

**a** Contrast Robert Reich's view of 'deregulation and flexibility' in the labour market with those of the Chancellor's. **(5)**

**b** Why did devaluation and lower interest rates stimulate employment? **(10)**

**c** According to the author, Europe is in need of 'Keynesian' policies in favour of public expenditure. Explain what the author is advocating. **(5)**

**d** There has been a tremendous growth in the number of part-time workers in the UK over recent years. How do you think this trend will affect the overall wage rates in the economy and the rate of inflation. Give reasons for your answers. **(5)**

## Student guide

### FREEDOM TO WORK IS NOT A PART-TIME PRINCIPLE

**1** Unfortunately this newspaper headline is not particularly helpful although the caption does focus your attention on the labour market.

**2** Read through the article carefully, jotting down relevant snippets of economic theory or making a simple summary.

| | |
|---|---|
| Paragraph 1 | Unemployment growth rate falling – good news! |
| Paragraph 2 | Deregulation and flexibility – UK: lower wages and more freedom for the boss; US: improving skills and mobility of workers. |
| Paragraph 3 | Fall in unemployment growth rate more the result of UK leaving ERM, pound floating down, lower interest rates. |
| Paragraph 4 | Fall in unemployment growth rate also helped by demographic trends (e.g. staying on at school). |
| Paragraph 5 | Reference again to the benefits of devaluation and lower interest rates on jobs – why? |
| Paragraph 6 | Still more people out of work – need more demand creating policies |
| Paragraph 7 | Use Keynesian spending plans to create more demand and lower unemployment. |

**3** Check the mark weightings carefully – don't waste time on questions which carry few marks.

**4** Read questions carefully and make sure you mix data with relevant economic theory in your answers.

**5** If you wish to use a diagram as part of your answer it must be accurate, well labelled and be referred to in your written answer.

# Minimum wage spells maximum harm

WALK INTO any branch of McDonald's in France, order the house speciality – a Big Mac, no fries – and the price will be roughly 45p more than that demanded at any McDonald's in the UK.

Part of the price difference is due to the strong French franc, but much of it can be blamed on the official minimum wage in France of £4.70 an hour. The French and the UK economies are growing at approximately the same rate, but unemployment in France is running at almost a third higher than that in the UK. That, in a nut-shell, is the truth about the minimum wages: it costs jobs.

Much debate is centring around the possibility of a minimum wage of £3.50 an hour in the UK. According to one survey a minimum wage at this level would affect 3.8 million workers – most of whom are women and the young, and many of whom are in part-time employment. Economists at Kleinwort Benson believe that the current average wage of these 3.8 million people is about £2.76 an hour and so a minimum wage of £3.50 would immediately boost spending power by 25% whilst adding £4 billion to the national wage bill. Of course, that is not the end of the story. The labour market in the UK is traditionally keen to maintain wage differentials and, so, the knock-on effect of a minimum wage in the region of £3.50 an hour might ultimately cause the final wage bill to rise by anything up to £11 billion.

The first round of job losses will follow as employers look for cost savings. Experience shows that the first to suffer will be the unskilled or low skilled and young workers who are not viewed as being worth the new minimum wage.

The fiscal boost given to the economy by the imposition of the minimum wage is likely to fuel inflation and bring about higher interest rates in an effort to contain it. Both would be damaging to the economy, while the impact on company profits could lead to a second round of job losses.

Economist Patrick Minford has estimated that the total job loss to the economy of a minimum wage of £3.50 could be as much as 1.4 million people. At the other end of the spectrum, Kleinwort Benson estimates the damage to be confined to some 200,000 jobs mainly in retailing, catering and the textile industry.

(Adapted from an article by Helen Dunne, The *Observer*, September 1995)

## Questions

**a** Using supply and demand analysis explain how a minimum wage might result in unemployment in the economy. **(4)**

**b** What is meant by 'wage differentials'? Explain why they might conceivably add to the wage bill. **(4)**

**c** Explain how higher wages might result in higher inflation rates. Why is it difficult to determine whether higher wages or other economic variables are causing the rate of inflation to increase? **(7)**

**d** Discuss the economic effects of higher interest rates on the economy. **(10)**

# Student guide

## MINIMUM WAGE SPELLS MAXIMUM HARM

**1** Note the title: you might have assumed that minimum wages in the economy were all to the good – not so!

**2** Read through each paragraph and summarise the economic content (if any!), trying to identify any relevant economic theory. For example:

| Paragraph 2 | Minimum wages costs jobs – demand and supply of labour analysis. |
| Paragraph 3 | Minimum wage affects young, women and part-timers – more spending power – inflation? Wage differentials – occupational wage ladder. |
| Paragraph 4 | Minimum wage – higher costs – get rid of workers. |
| Paragraph 5 | Higher wages, higher spending, inflation . . . interest rates to curb demand. |
| Paragraph 6 | Unemployment could rise by anything between 200,000 and 1.4 million. |

**3** Check the mark weightings – don't waste time on questions which do not warrant it!

**4** Remember to mix relevant economic theory with extracted data.

**5** Diagrams are always useful if adequately explained and must obviously be accurate and well labelled.

**6** Introduce some current economic perspective/history if possible.

# A recovery faltering through lack of investment

ONCE UPON A TIME, a long time ago, economic policy was dominated by the desire to maintain full employment. Today, as growth slows and unemployment begins to rise again, the Treasury declares itself 'delighted' with the economy's performance. The government's ambition does not seem to extend beyond a growth rate of 2.5% per year and a permanent level of unemployment above 2.3 million people.

Whatever happened to the so called 'recovery'? Some clues are to be found in two OECD reports published recently. In one report it has been stated that the widely held belief that the devaluation of the pound in September 1992 sparked off the export boom of 1994 and heralded in a new era of competitive export-led growth – *is without foundation*. In fact the OECD report goes on to show that Britain's exports over the period 1992–94 grew no faster than the growth of the markets into which they were sold. Plainly speaking, British markets captured no extra market share *despite the devaluation*. Further, the report explains that import performance has fared no better. The share of imports in Britain's home market fell during the early 1990s, but today it is far greater than in 1992 *despite the devaluation* of the pound.

So the devaluation of the pound in 1992 has not led to competitive growth in both markets at home and abroad. In spite of these adverse trends, the balance of payments has managed to improve substantially – simply since markets overseas grew faster than markets at home.

The second OECD report published recently seems at odds with itself. The textual part of the report congratulates the UK's 1994 performance and suggests that the economy has been made more flexible, competitive and less inflation-prone as a result of *'structural reform'* launched in the 1980s. However, the statistical analysis does not back up the almost elated text. Not only do the statistics confirm the truth behind the UK's trade performance, but also they make clear that business investment has failed to increase at all during the so-called 'recovery'. This is in marked contrast to levels of investment during the recovery from the last Tory depression. Two-and-a-half years after the 1981 recessional trough, investment was 20% up – today business investment has barely increased from its 1992 level.

Personal consumption growth and booming export markets can keep a recovery going for a short while. But with overseas growth slowing down and no competitive increase in the market share, that stimulus is petering out. Meanwhile, investment – the driving force of competitiveness and the ultimate anti-inflationary weapon, has grown not at all.

Without higher investment, the economy is trapped in endless low growth and high unemployment, alleviated by the occasional expansionary 'blip'. Without higher investment Britain cannot hope to compete with countries such as France and Germany which, year after year, devote 5% more of their national income to investment, or Japan, which invests a huge 12% more.

It is to investment that the government must urgently turn its attention.

(Adapted from an article by Helen Dunne, The *Observer*, September 1995)

## Questions

**a** How would you explain the 'widely held belief' that a devaluation of the pound, such as that in September 1992, might conceivably result in 'a new era of competitive export-led growth'? **(4)**

**b** What sort of 'structural reforms' took place in the 1980s and might have made the economy more 'flexible, competitive and less inflation-prone'? **(8)**

**c** Explain why business investment might be considered as 'the driving force of competitiveness and the ultimate anti-inflationary weapon'. **(6)**

**d** What policies do you think the government might consider in an attempt to increase the level of private investment? **(7)**

---

# Student guide

### A RECOVERY FALTERING THROUGH LACK OF INVESTMENT

1 The headline is helpful in this case – it is suggesting that our economic performance is being limited by lack of investment in capital goods.

2 As you read this newspaper article take special notice of the words and phrases in italics – these will almost certainly be key aspects in the questions.

| | |
|---|---|
| Paragraph 1 | Are we accepting higher levels of unemployment? |
| Paragraph 2 | Devaluation of pound after UK left ERM did not result in any marked improvement in exports and imports no better. |
| Paragraph 4 | Contradiction in two OECD reports – one suggests that 1980s structural reforms (supply-side economics) have been very successful; other report emphasises the lack of UK investment. |
| Paragraph 5 | Emphasises that lack of investment is a real problem in UK. |
| Paragraph 6 | Without the investment UK cannot compete with other countries. |

3 Read through the article carefully, making summary notes or reference to economic theory. For example:

4 Read the questions carefully and check the mark weightings – don't spend too much time on questions which carry few marks to the detriment of others that are more valuable.

5 Remember to mix data with relevant economic theory.

6 Read the questions through carefully, making sure that you understand key commands such as 'explain' or 'analyse'.

# Unemployment

THERE CAN BE no doubt who is the current superstar among economic policy makers – Steady Eddie, the Hard Man of Threadneedle Street, also known as the Governor of the Bank of England. As the result of the new 'policy openness' which now exists between the Treasury and the Chancellor, Mr Clarke, the Chancellor, must, and does, listen to Mr George.

The Governor's economic views were clearly set out recently in a powerful lecture. His position is clear and precise: 'By almost any reckoning a large part of the present level of total unemployment is structural. That means it is beyond the present reach of macro-eco-nomic policy, and is unlikely to disappear as a result of the present cyclical expansion.'

The Governor therefore believes that active monetary or fiscal policy to reduce unemployment would 'be likely to make things worse in anything but the short term'. At the core of the Governor's economics is the basic proposition that there exists a 'natural' rate of unemployment, and 'the results of trying to reduce unemployment below this natural rate are unstable and potentially explosive for inflation'.

So what is the UK's natural rate of unemployment? The Governor quotes the OECD estimate of 8–8.5%. This is only one half of a percentage point below where the UK economy is now. No wonder the Governor believes that macro-economic policy can make only a limited contribution to reducing unemployment. All this is commendably frank, as are the Governor's proposals to reduce the natural rate, namely enhancing the 'flexibility and competitiveness of industry'.

The main difficulty here is that the concept of the natural rate is extremely shaky. If there is such a thing, it doesn't stay put. It tends to drift upwards in times of high unemployment and downwards in times of lower unemployment.

(Adapted from The *Observer*, January 1995)

## Questions

a  Compare and contrast cyclical unemployment with structural unemployment. **(10)**

b  Explain why the Governor of the Bank of England is wary of trying to reduce the present level of unemployment below its 'natural' level. **(10)**

c  Evidence suggests that the natural level of unemployment in the UK economy is actually increasing. Why do you think this is so? **(5)**

# Student guide

**UNEMPLOYMENT**

1  There is not much to be gained from this headline!

2  Read through the newspaper article carefully, jotting down relevant economic theory or summary points, where appropriate. For example:

| Paragraph 1 | Chancellor and Governor meet regularly to discuss economic policy. |
| --- | --- |
| Paragraph 2 | Governor thinks UK is suffering badly from structural unemployment – major problem is old-fashioned industries and workers inflexible to new technology. |
| Paragraph 3 | Structural unemployment can't be solved by demand-stimulating policies – leads to inflation. Natural level of unemployment – diagram? |
| Paragraph 4 | Deal with structural unemployment by increasing flexibility and competitiveness – supply-side economics? |

3  Check mark weightings – do not waste time on questions which carry insufficient marks.

4  Read questions carefully and mix theory with data.

5  Include a relevant diagram which must be well labelled and referred to in your written answer.

## Data 26: The M&S of water – a step ahead of demand

**a** The text book definition of a *monopoly* is that it is the sole producer of a good for which there are no close substitutes. Clearly, such a definition would make for a perfectly inelastic demand curve. The working definition of a *monopolist* used by the Monopolies and Mergers Commission is that it is a company or enterprise which has at least 25% of the 'market share'. Such a definition would still give rise to a relatively inelastic demand curve confronting the company. In either case, consumer choice is limited under monopolistic conditions particularly as monopolists, by definition, must somehow be able to 'keep out' new entrants from the industry. It is this lack of choice for the consumer which enables the company to abuse the consumer in terms of high prices for sometimes poor quality goods or services.

The data provided, however, makes it clear that not all monopolies act in this manner and, indeed, competition policy in the UK judges monopoly companies on their own merits or demerits rather than making blanket judgements.

**b** Welsh Water, like most businesses, imposes some adverse externalities onto the community in the form of river and waterway pollution. However, like most companies, it is more concerned with its private production costs – manpower, sewerage treatment plants, technology costs – rather than these external costs. The Environment Agency is now regulating the industry much more carefully than previously and is forcing it to deal with its adverse externalities.

In terms of the diagram opposite we see that in a free market Welsh Water would charge $P_1$ for $Q_1$ service – the result of demand, $D_1$, and marginal private costs of MPC. Yet this market equilibrium ignores the adverse externalities imposed on the community. The full social costs which are equal to private costs + adverse externalities (or minus any positive externalities) is given by the marginal social costs curve, MSC and therefore to cover social costs Welsh Water must charge $P_2$ for $Q_2$ service. The extra charge to the consumer will yield the neces-

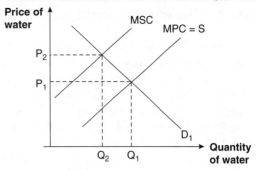

MPC = Marginal private cost
MSC = Marginal social cost

sary revenue which Welsh Water needs to cope with the stringent regulations laid down by the Environment Agency.

**c** The data suggests that efficiency since privatisation has increased in a number of ways. The most obvious reference is to the slimming down of the organisation in terms of manpower from 4,000 workers to 3,000 workers and presumably the service has not suffered in response. There is also a clear reference to the organisation leading the way in 'environmental cleaning up'. Although this might initially involve extra expense for the business there is the likelihood of recouping those expenses in the future. Apart from anything else, being environmentally friendly is a good marketing strategy.

The data also suggests that consumer charges will not increase at the expected 5.5% above the inflation rate as once predicted; instead charges would rise at 0.5% above inflation due to the gain in efficiency over the past five years. Although much of this can be attributable to the savings in labour already discussed there might have been further cost saving gains in terms of plant and technology.

**d** Welsh Water is now in the private sector owned by shareholders who expect a dividend on their investments. If the business does not look after its customers, then those customers will look elsewhere for the service or, at least, reduce their demand for the service. Either way, profitability can be adversely affected and dividends to shareholders lowered. Share values might then fall and at this stage a hostile take-over bid may then occur – affecting shareholders' interests.

# Answers

## Data 27: The effective exchange rate

**a** A single currency exchange rate is the value of one currency against another currency. For instance £1 might exchange at $1.5. The effective exchange rate is the value of one currency against a range of currencies and so is a truer reflection of the worth of a currency on worldwide markets. The effective exchange rate is usually given in an index form and the calculation of it takes into account the relative weights of each of the currencies in the 'basket' according to the proportion of trade undertaken with that country.

**b** One might expect that the balance of payments on current account and the effective exchange rate might have a direct relationship although some time lag might exist. Assuming freely floating exchange rates, theory suggests that the value of a currency is determined by the market forces of supply and demand for various currencies. If a balance of payments surplus exists then it tends to imply that the export market is strong and the import market weak. As a result, the demand for sterling increases as foreigners exchange their dollars into sterling to pay their debts, whilst simultaneously the supply of sterling onto the market diminishes since UK residents have less need to change their sterling into dollars to pay for imports. The result is an appreciation in the international value of sterling as illustrated below.

Thus balance of payment surpluses on current account should be closely followed by

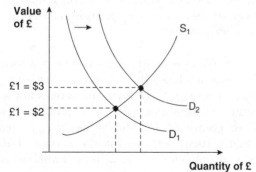

D₁ = Original demand for £
S₁ = Original supply of £
D₂ = New demand for £

appreciation of the effective exchange rate and deficits should be closely followed by depreciation of the effective exchange rate. There is some evidence in the data to suggest that this relationship might be true. For instance, from 1973 to 1976 the current account was in deficit and in the same period the effective value of sterling was depreciating. In the period 1976–84 the current account moved into surplus and although the effective exchange initially appreciated, by 1981 it was already depreciating. That depreciation continued, even though the current account did not move into deficit until 1984. Clearly, the relationship does not seem to be close, suggesting that other factors are at work in influencing the effective exchange rate.

**c** There would seem to be other factors at working influencing the effective exchange rate. On the one hand, and the evidence is supportive in this instance, the rate of interest in the economy is important. If interest rates are relatively high in the UK, 'hot' money will flow into the UK to take advantage of the higher rewards. The demand for sterling therefore rises and so the effective exchange will rise.

Speculation in currencies, especially when the exchange rate is freely floating, very much influences the international value of a currency. Speculators make their profit by buying and selling currencies at appropriate times. The speculative market is very much dependent on anticipation and hunches – if speculators can 'foresee' economic problems ahead for a certain economy they will act now by selling that currency and buying into a much safer currency. Therefore speculation is a very powerful force on the effective exchange rate.

As far as the UK economy is concerned, the value of sterling is also dependent upon the price of oil on world markets. Sterling is a petrocurrency reflecting the importance of North Sea oil production in the economy. In situations where the world price of oil is increasing we can expect to see an upward movement in the effective exchange rate. Therefore information regarding the price of oil on world markets might be useful.

## Data 28: The Utopian economy

a A consumption function relates household consumption to either total income or to disposable income – other things remaining constant. The Utopian consumption function is given by the equation:

C = 2000 + 0.8Y$_d$

therefore even at zero disposable income, autonomous consumption is 2000. (Utopian households must be dis-saving to sustain their consumption.) As disposable income rises so the proportion of disposable income spent is a constant 0.8; £8 out of every £10 is spent on consumption. This proportion is better known as the marginal propensity to consume (MPC). Since the MPC is a constant 0.8 it implies that the consumption function itself has a constant slope of 0.8. The consumption function is illustrated below:

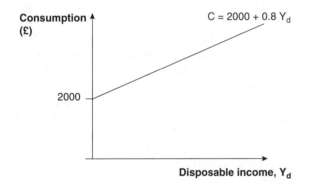

b *Equilibrium national income* refers to a situation where the level of income/expenditure/output in the Utopian economy is not prone to change. This will occur when the withdrawals out of the circular flow of income are just equal to the injections into the circular flow. In this simple economy the only withdrawals are savings and taxation and the only injections are government expenditure on goods and services and private investment.

Therefore, at equilibrium:

S + T = I + G

where S = –2000 + 0.272Y$_d$ and Y$_d$ = 0.75Y$_t$

so, S = –2000 + 0.15Y$_t$

Also T = 0.25Y$_t$, I = 800 and G = 3,200

Hence,

–2,000 + 0.15Y$_t$ + 0.25Y$_t$ = 800 + 3,200

0.4Y$_t$ = 4,000 + 2,000

Y$_t$ = 6,000 × 0.4 = 15,000

Note: S is savings, T is taxation, I is investment and G is government spending.

Therefore, the equilibrium level of national income for Utopia is £15,000 billion.

c In order to bring about full employment the Utopian government needs to create £1,000 billion by increasing its own expenditure on goods and services directly. When the government increases its expenditure there will be a multiplier effect in the Utopian economy.

The value of the multiplier is given by:

$$\frac{1}{MPS + MPT}$$

where MPS is the marginal propensity to save

= 0.2 × 0.75 = 0.15.

where MPT is the marginal propensity to be taxed

= 0.25.

Therefore the multiplier has the value of:

$$\frac{1}{0.15 + 0.25} = 2.5$$

Therefore, given the multiplier value of 2.5, the government must spend a further £400 billion in the Utopian economy to create the necessary £1,000 billion of national income which will eliminate the unemployment.

d With the initial equilibrium national income of £15,000 billion the government was spending £3,200 billion and raising taxes of 0.25 of £15,000. Therefore, the tax revenue raised was £3,750 and the government's budget was a surplus of £550 billion. The new level of national income is £16,000 billion and the government spending has risen to £3,600. Taxation revenue is now 0.25 of £16,000 billion which is £400 billion. The Utopian government's budget is now in surplus to the tune of £400 billion.

# Answers

## Data 29: Bankers declare war on the currency dealers

**a** Dealers have managed to push the yen and the mark to such 'dizzy heights' by creating a huge increase in the demand for such currencies (and conversely supplying dollars on the market in order to purchase the yen and the mark). Speculation by dealers in currency is certainly the main cause of exchange rate volatility, in the short term at least. Speculators anticipating a rise in the value of a certain currency will increase their demand for that currency and thus help bring their anticipations into fruition.

The effect of speculation is shown in the diagrams at the bottom of the page which show what happens when speculators move into the yen and out of the dollar.

**b** The triple alliance between the Japanese, the German and the American central banks has successfully managed to push the dollar back up and bring the other two currencies down in value. By collectively purchasing dollars on the foreign exchange market (and collectively selling the yen and the mark) the three central banks have been acting in opposition to the dealers/speculators *with greater success*. The alliance, obviously, requires a pool of currencies in order to manipulate international currency values.

**c** The Bank of England is referring to the herd behaviour of dealers in the sense that speculators closely follow the actions of others and if they are more successful they will follow a similar course of action. In this case, the speculators realised that the triple alliance was determined to push up the value of the dollar and bring down the yen and the mark and that there was little point in speculating further against the dollar. Dealers eventually responded by buying the more profitable dollar themselves – hence securing its upward rise.

**d** The dollar weakness over the last decade has largely been the result of the US budget deficit and balance of payments deficit. A budget deficit suggests that the government is spending more than it is raising in revenue. One of the likely outcomes of a continual budget deficit is a high rate of inflation which in turn results in a depreciation of the external exchange rate. Further, the low tax rates and the high government spending can suck in imports giving rise to the balance of payments deficit which, again, will have a tendency to keep the value of the dollar low. Only when the budget deficit and the balance of payments deficit reduces will the value of the dollar begin to climb.

The data suggests that there is evidence of this reversal now in operation in the US economy. The budget deficit is now less than 2% of GDP. Further, the US trade deficit, particularly with Japan, is showing signs of reversal.

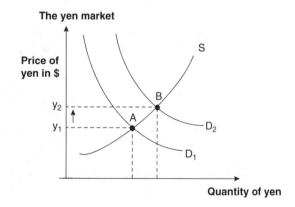

*The yen appreciates*

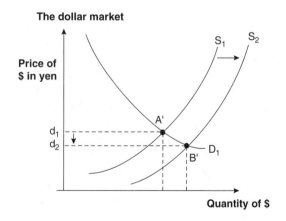

*The dollar depreciates*

# Answers

## Data 30: Dairy farms go down the drain

**a** The EU system of farm support relies basically on setting guaranteed prices to farmers which are often above the free market price. As a result, there is a surplus of the product which the EU must buy up and stockpile in order to prevent the price falling below its guaranteed level to the free market price. These stockpiles have been highlighted by the so-called beef mountains, wine lakes and butter mountains, etc.

The original system intended, of course, that in poor years when harvests were depleted, the stockpiles should be released on the market to prevent the market price rising too far above the guaranteed level. However, it has been the case that European harvests are rarely sufficiently poor to allow the stockpiles onto the European market.

European farmers, safe in the knowledge that the EU will always buy up surplus products, have a tendency to overproduce – making the surpluses and the stockpiles a very real and expensive embarrassment for the EU agricultural policy. Quotas were introduced in an attempt to place limits on milk production, therefore reducing the scale of the surpluses. This is shown diagrammatically as follows:

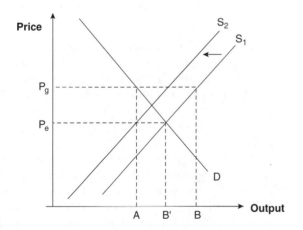

The guaranteed price of $P_g$ which is above the natural equilibrium of $P_e$ results in a stockpile of AB. The introduction of the quota forces the supply curve to shift to the left to position $S_2$ and the size of the surplus therefore falls to AB'.

**b** The trading price of the milk quotas has risen substantially for two reasons. First, the Milk Marketing Board has been disbanded in the UK and instead several dairy companies have taken the initiative. The free market is forcing up the price of the quota – especially as many people see the quota as an investment without having to be actually involved in the farming industry.

Secondly, a mild autumn has resulted in extra milk production and farmers' quotas have been used up quickly this year. The cattle continue to produce the milk, despite the quota being completed. Farmers are therefore willing to purchase unused quotas from other farmers at inflated prices rather than actually throw the milk down the drain.

**c** The milk quotas would seem to be a very good investment in the sense that at the moment their value is high because of the increased demand for unused quotas. The data provides plenty of evidence that retired farmers who still own the land but not the herds are certainly benefiting from the sale of their unused quotas. However, like any other investment the quotas are a risk. It is possible for the EU to increase the scale of the quota and many farmers will then have purchased the quotas at a higher price than their current value. Reform in the EU system of farm support might certainly affect the investment nature of the milk quota.

### Data 31: Don't shoot the economist

**a** Perfect competition is a market structure which has certain characteristics. These are:

* There are a large number of companies in the market such that individually no one company can influence the market price by changing its output. The market price is given to the companies and they are said to be price-takers although they have the ability, obviously, to change their own prices.

* The product sold by each and every company in the market is homogeneous. This means that the product or service is identical to that supplied by all the other companies in the industry. Consumers therefore are able to buy the product from one of very many companies. Since the product is homogeneous, consumers will react to even minute price variations in the market.

* There is freedom of entry and exit into the industry. Companies are attracted into the industry by the existence of abnormal profit and feel forced to leave the industry when less than normal profit is made.

* There is free and full information available for both consumers and producers. Producers are well aware of their rivals' pricing and output decisions and consumers are aware of variations in price in any part of the country.

Clearly the model of perfect competition is very much hypothetical. Homogeneity of product and services is very far from the truth; companies go to great expense to differentiate their products and services, if not in their composition then by advertising. Similarly there is not free and full information available for both consumers and producers. Companies do not reveal their marketing and output strategies to their rivals and clearly consumers are not fully aware of price differences regionally. Even the assumption concerning freedom of entry and exit into the industry is contentious. Many markets are regulated by the government; others are dominated by large powerful companies which prevent new entrants by both legal means and by erecting other barriers to entry.

**b** Perfectly competitive markets give rise to an ideal state of society at two levels. First, competition between rival companies will eventually secure resource allocative efficiency where the price of the product will be equal to the marginal cost of production. This is illustrated in the long-term equilibrium diagram for a perfectly competitive company, as shown below:

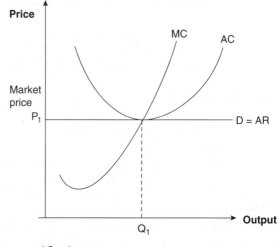

AC = Average cost

MC = Marginal cost

MR = Marginal revenue

AR = Average revenue

The profit maximising company will produce $Q_1$ at the market price of $P_1$ – where marginal cost is equal to marginal revenue. In the long term, freedom of entry and exit will ensure that only normal profits are made – where average revenue is equal to average costs.

Notice that at $Q_1$ the marginal production costs are equal to the price at which the good is sold, $P_1$. Consumers want no more and no less of this good and society has a perfect resource allocation. In addition, production of $Q_1$ occurs at the minimum point of the average cost curve – indicating productive efficiency for society. $Q_1$ is said to be the optimal level of production.

**c** If demand for a certain product or service is price 'elastic' then it implies that a change in price is followed by a larger change in the quantity demanded. The price elasticity co-efficient is greater than −1. Therefore, if the price of a good increases by, say, 5% the subsequent fall in demand is more than 5% and the total revenue to the company – price × number sold – will fall. This proposition is shown graphically as follows:

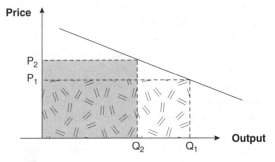

 Original total revenue = $TR_1 = P_1 \times Q_1$

New total revenue = $TR_2 = P_2 \times Q_2$

**d** There are many answers which are applicable here and credit should be awarded for technically correct economic theory supported with a relevant example. For example, reference may be made to:

* the principle of substitution and its implication for the resource mix
* price elasticity of demand and supply, and implications for indirect taxation
* maximum/minimum price imposition and the effect on labour market/agriculture
* the effect of interest rates on the propensity to invest
* the effect of changes in the value of sterling on import costs and export competitiveness.

### Data 32: Freedom to work is not a part-time principle

**a** Reich's view of deregulation and flexibility is to improve the skills of the workforce and to increase the mobility of labour. This will cause the supply of labour to shift rightwards and in theory will result in a lower level of unemployment at a lower market wage.

The Chancellor's view, according to Reich, is to have the 'freedom to fire people and reduce their wages'. In other words, without the protection of unions, employers are able to alter their workforces at will and force lower wages upon those 'lucky' enough to remain in employment.

**b** In the early 1990s the UK was committed to the fixed exchange rate mechanism of the ERM. For most of the period the pound was under continual pressure to depreciate – many would argue that we entered the system at an unrealistically high par value. To maintain the value of sterling the UK government was forced to keep domestic interest rates at a very high level. This created a sufficient demand for sterling on the foreign exchange market to maintain par value but the opportunity cost of high interest rates in the domestic economy was recession – as consumers reduced their demand for goods and services, and producers ran into cash flow problems.

The devaluation of sterling in September 1992 greatly alleviated the recession. On the one hand, the devaluation resulted in an improvement in the UK competitive situation against other countries creating more jobs in the export markets. In addition, the devaluation of sterling meant that the government was not forced to hold interest rates up – as interest rates began to fall, so consumer demand picked up and producers found that they were able to invest in new equipment and so forth, both of which reduced the level of unemployment.

**c** Keynesian policies to reduce unemployment refer to the government increasing its direct expenditure on goods and services which will then be multiplied throughout the economy according to the value of the 'multiplier'. If, for example, the government increases its expenditure on road building by £10 billion, then initially workers engaged in road construction will gain employment and the £10 billion will filter into the pockets of these people – surveyors and manual workers – through to the shareholders of companies such as Mowlem and Costain.

The effect on the economy doesn't stop here. The vast majority of the £10 billion will be spent on domestically produced goods and services, although some will be saved, some removed in the form of taxation and some spent on imports. By spending on UK goods and services the first generation of recipients creates income and work for a wide range of other people – waiters, car manufacturers, hairdressers and so on. The initial £10 billion ends up creating national income or wealth to a much greater value. This is the multiplier at work.

**d** The trend for more and more part-time workers will tend to depress the national average wage since part-time workers tend to be paid at a lower hourly rate than full-time workers. The main reason for this is that many part-time workers are women and also older members of the workforce who traditionally are prepared to work for lower wages. In addition, part-time workers are very often not in a trade union which is able to support its members in their wage claims. Lower wages will cause the aggregate supply curve to shift to the left as production costs fall, and in turn this will help to reduce the rate of inflation – assuming inflation to be cost-push in nature.

## Answers

### Data 33: Minimum wage spells maximum harm

**a** In the diagram below $D_1$ refers to the demand for labour and $S_1$ refers to the supply of labour at various wage rates. The equilibrium wage rate in the market would tend to be $W_e$ where the demand for labour is just equal to the supply of labour. Assume now that the government imposes a minimum wage of $W_{min}$ onto the market – what will happen? On the one hand, the supply of labour increases from n to n' – the higher wage rate tempts more individuals to search for paid employment. On the other hand, the demand for workers now falls from n to n" – companies can no longer afford to employ the more expensive labour.

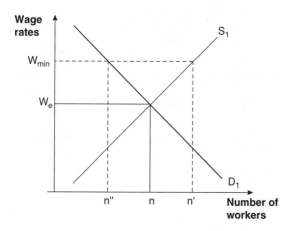

The total unemployment in the economy is that represented by n"n' and some of the unemployed are individuals who once held a job at the equilibrium wage (n"n). These individuals are certainly no better off through the imposition of the minimum wage – they are now unemployed. The data is suggesting that unemployment in France is currently running at almost one-third higher than that in the UK because of the imposition of minimum wages. Only those individuals lucky enough to retain their employment have benefited from the minimum wage.

**b** The UK labour market is characterised by an adherence to wage differentials. Simply, there exists a occupational ladder of wage rewards which workers cling to quite fiercely. We expect doctors to be paid more than teachers and we equally expect teachers to be paid more than shop assistants who in turn get paid more than road sweepers. Should one occupation receive a pay award, sometimes quite justifiably, there is a knock-on effect for pay awards in other occupations – particularly those on the next rung of the ladder. The data are suggesting that although a minimum wage might be imposed to help those on very low wages, the final effect of the total wage bill will be much greater as other occupations seek to retain their differentials.

**c** Wages are a major cost of production for most companies and the effect of higher wage rates in the economy is likely to affect the rate of inflation as illustrated in the diagram below.

The economy is in macro-equilibrium where the aggregate supply curve $AS_1$ is equal to the aggregate demand curve $AD_1$ giving rise to an output/employment level $Q_1$ and an inflation rate of $P_1$.

As wage rates rise, so the aggregate supply curve shifts leftwards to $AS_2$ and all things remaining constant a partial macro-equilibrium establishes itself at $Q_2$ and $P_2$. Initially, there is some adjustment in both employment levels and inflation rates. However,

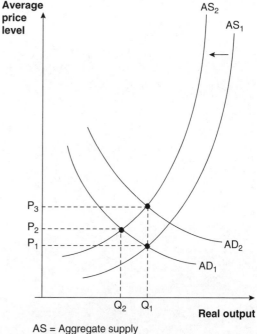

AS = Aggregate supply
AD= Aggregate demand

103

the increased wage will eventually show itself in an increase in aggregate demand as individuals decide to increase their consumption – $AD_1$ shifts to $AD_2$. The final macro-equilibrium is therefore at $Q_1$ and $P_3$. Full adjustment is in the fore of rapidly rising price levels.

Although it might seem comparatively easy to determine whether the cause of inflation is rising wages rather than any other economic variable, in practice this is not so. Many economists would argue that the cause of inflation could well be buoyant and rising demand or perhaps excessive increases in the money supply, or even increases in the cost of imported raw materials. The problem is that all these variables, including wage costs, tend to rise together during inflationary periods and it is very difficult to isolate one of many variables as the actual instigator of the rise in inflation.

**d** Higher interest rates to contain the rate of inflation caused by the imposition of the minimum wage can have several effects. Politically, the government might find them embarrassing. Externally, the higher interest rates in the UK might attract 'hot' money into the country looking for a good reward. As the demand for sterling increases so will its international value. A strong pound will cause the price of imports to fall whilst the price of exports will rise. Many of these imports will be raw materials and hence cheaper materials should result in lower prices for finished goods – inflation begins to fall. At the same time, goods which once would have been sold on export markets now become available for domestic consumption and again this will tend to depress price levels.

Internally, the higher interest rates will cause a fall in consumption and investment expenditure. Lower aggregate demand will also have the effect of reducing the rate of inflation. However, there is an opportunity cost – as aggregate demand decreases so job losses will be inevitable.

Finally, it should be noted that higher interest rates will affect future economic growth since they tend to diminish investment – the prerequisite of growth.

# Answers

## Data 34: A recovery faltering through lack of investment

**a**  A *devaluation* (depreciation) of the pound refers to a situation in which the value of sterling is falling on the foreign exchange markets. As a result, the price of imports rises whilst the price of exports falls. Providing the combined price elasticity of demand for imports and exports is greater than –1, the devaluation should improve the overall trading position of the economy and achieve a move towards a more favourable balance of payments position. In September 1992, the UK left the fixed exchange rate regime of the ERM and sterling floated downwards resulting theoretically, at least, in a new era of export led growth.

**b**  The structural reforms of the 1980s can be collectively described as supply-side economics with the aim of shifting the aggregate supply curve to the right and resulting in higher levels of output, but lower inflation rates. This can be illustrated diagrammatically as follows:

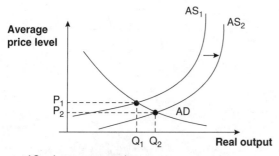

AS = Aggregate supply
AD = Aggregate demand

One main area of reform was in the area of marginal taxation at both individual and corporate level. Reductions in marginal rates were intended to create an incentive to work and to save at an individual level and through reductions in corporation tax an incentive for companies to invest. The outcome of this was to improve competition and simultaneously to reduce inflationary pressures by making more goods and services available.

Labour reforms in the 1980s concentrated on freeing the labour market of restrictions in the form of trade unions and nationally agreed wage levels. In addition, more emphasis on vocational training in the workplace and in schools was hoped to improve flexibility in the workforce.

*Deregulation* refers to the removal of government regulations on activities of the business sector which normally serve to restrict competition. In the 1980s, deregulation of the Stock Exchange, bus services, school meals and much more opened up competition in these areas.

Finally, privatisation was a major structural reform in the 1980s. *Privatisation* was a method in which share ownership could be widened and hopefully deepened in order to provide more funds for industrial investment. Privatisation also forced organisations and businesses to become more efficient since government support (from the taxpayer) is removed following privatisation.

**c**  *Investment* is the acquisition of capital goods to increase productive capacity. Investment causes the aggregate supply curve to shift outwards – thereby reducing inflation and raising output. Correspondingly, investment seeks to increase national income (by an amount determined by the value of the multiplier) and therefore employment opportunities.

Investment in the form of hi-tech developments is very important in consumer markets and without that development export markets will diminish. The data suggests that France, Japan and Germany consistently devote more of their national income to investment and unless the UK makes that same commitment it cannot hope to compete.

**d**  Government policies to increase investment levels in the UK would seem to be a priority. First, the government could consider reducing the rate of interest which would not only stimulate investment, but also personal consumption. Secondly, although the relationship between investment and interest rates is well documented in the marginal efficiency of capital theory, it is sufficient to note that lower interest rates make the cost of borrowing cheaper and therefore, since much investment is undertaken by using borrowed funds, the volume of investment should increase.

Tax advantages for investment should be considered as a policy to promote investment – although it should be made clear whether the tax advantage is for new investment or simply replacement investment. Similarly, lower corporation tax rates will allow companies to finance their investments through their own internal sources and this policy might be pursued.

Small companies often find themselves starved of investment funds and perhaps the government might consider ways and means in which finance might be made available to both high-risk ventures and the smaller company. One might wish to consider the availability of government grants and subsidies to selected industries which invest in environmentally 'clean' technology.

**Note:** credit could be awarded to the interpretation of investment in 'human capital' through more effective education and training facilities.

## Answers

### Data 35: Unemployment

**a** *Cyclical unemployment* is unemployment associated with the trade cycle with its alternating periods of rising and falling aggregate demand. It is, in fact, often described as demand-deficiency unemployment. Most OECD countries have experienced a period of falling output in the late 1980s and early 1990s – this is commonly known as 'the recession'. Companies have simply found their markets shrinking and have responded by either slimming down their workforce to cut costs or by going out of business altogether. Cyclical unemployment is, however, a temporary form of unemployment and as the recovery gets under way via demand-stimulating policies such as low interest rates, low levels of personal taxation and higher levels of government expenditure, so employment opportunities will resume.

*Structural unemployment* is altogether more serious and is unlikely to respond to demand-stimulating policies. Structural unemployment is a long-term problem and evidence suggests that it is getting worse. Simply, it refers to a permanent problem with the supply of labour outweighing the demand for labour. Technological change seems to be one major cause of structural unemployment. However, the problem is not so much the fact that technology is replacing workers, but the fact that those workers displaced are not able to adapt sufficiently well to the employment opportunities which actually arise through the introduction of new technology. A second explanation of structural unemployment concerns trade. It is often said that imports from low wage, less developed countries are undercutting domestically produced goods giving rise to structural unemployment. However, trade is 'good for all' when pursued along lines of comparative advantage. Trade does not destroy jobs, but it does create pressure for change in the economy.

Generally speaking, policies designed to reduce structural unemployment centre on improving the efficiency of markets and in particular improving the flexibility of the labour market – commonly known as supply-side policies – by privatisation, trade union reform, deregulation, and reduction of marginal tax rates.

**b** The natural rate of unemployment can be viewed as the level of unemployment which the economy will gravitate to in the long term. At this 'equilibrium' level of unemployment those out of work are voluntarily so, ie they have chosen not to work. Therefore the natural level of unemployment is synonymous with full employment!

The Governor of the Bank of England would seem very wary of attempting to reduce the level of unemployment below its natural rate – 'the results of trying to reduce unemployment below this natural rate are unstable and potentially explosive for inflation'. The Governor is presumably referring to the 'expectations augmented Phillips curve' which can be illustrated as shown in the diagram below.

$U_1$ refers to the natural level of unemployment where the actual and expected rate of inflation is 0%. What happens when the government attempts to reduce the level of unemployment by using demand stimulating policies? In the short term, aggregate demand will increase and unemployment will begin to fall. However, the increased demand will soon start to put pressure on prices to rise. For a while the economy suffers from money illusion in the sense that individuals still expect the rate of inflation to be 0% and are unaware that price levels are beginning to increase. Individuals fail to recognise that their real incomes are in fact falling rather than rising. Demand continues to expand and prices

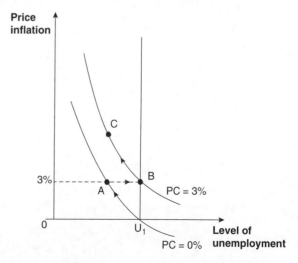

*The expectations augmented Phillips curve*

continue to rise. The economy is moving from $U_1$ to A along the short-term Phillips curve with expected inflation of 0%.

Eventually, individuals begin to realise that the increased prices are eroding their spending power and that real incomes are, in fact, falling. Manufacturers start to lay off workers and some members of the workforce voluntarily quit their jobs, preferring to be unemployed rather than work for a low real wage rate. In the long term, the economy floats back to position B – the natural level of unemployment has returned, but now inflation is running at 3%. Any further attempts to reduce the level of unemployment below its natural level will succeed only in the short term. In the long term, there is no trade-off between the rate of inflation and unemployment. Indeed, demand-stimulating policies for reducing unemployment can be potentially explosive for inflation.

c  There is evidence that the natural rate of unemployment is increasing in the UK economy over time. The reasons for this are several. First, there has been a growing mismatch between the demand for labour and the supply of labour. Net job losses have been fairly concentrated outside the south of England and have been mainly in male manufacturing whilst the new jobs coming on stream have been in the south, mainly in the service sector and are generally female oriented.

Secondly the UK's loss of competitiveness in foreign markets has contributed to the rise in the natural level of unemployment. High wage costs, and unrealistically strong values of sterling, have resulted in a marked deterioration in our exports.

A lack of aggregate demand has also contributed to the higher level of natural unemployment – simply there is insufficient demand to maintain employment levels. Without buoyant demand there is little point in maintaining a labour force.

A final consideration concerns government fiscal policy. Unemployment benefit rose in proportion to average wages making it more attractive for workers to remain unemployed. Simultaneously, employment taxes such as employers' National Insurance contributions have risen substantially, resulting in employers being less likely to employ as many workers as in the past.

# SECTION D: CASE STUDIES

# A step forward for health care?

> **This case study contains the following data:**
>
> Data 36A  The production possibility frontier for the West Midshire Trust Hospital
>
> Data 36B  A free market approach to health care
>
> Data 36C  Squeeze on tobacco users continues
>
> Data 36D  The relationship between smoking and prices
>
> Examine all the following data before answering the questions.

## Data 36A: Production possibility frontier for the West Midshire Trust Hospital (weekly)

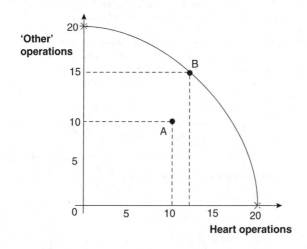

## Data 36B: A free market approach to health care

Some economists argue that the free market, whereby consumers pay the market price for their medical attention, would deliver the best possible health care at the lowest possible cost *providing* the authorities can introduce competition into the market place. That means ensuring that the medical profession do not operate restrictive practices in the provision of health care. Effective competition will result in an allocation of medical services to the community which is both allocative and productive efficient.

The greater choice created by the free market will cause producers of health care to become more responsive to consumer demands, resulting in a move towards allocative efficiency. The medical profession will produce services which consumers want and are willing to pay for – what better allocation of scarce resources can there be? Another result of increasing competition will be a significant fall in costs as medical services respond to falling consumer demand – brought about by having to pay for health care – by becoming much more cost-conscious. Doctors' real incomes could be the first cost-cutting exercise introduced by the free market health care industry.

Such arguments seem strong when compared to the current state provision of the National Health Service.

## Data 36C

# Squeeze on tobacco users continues

By Celia Hall, Medical Editor

**THE PRICE of cigarettes has been increased above the rate of inflation for the third year running as part of the drive to get smokers to quit.**

An extra 15p will be put on a packet of 20 cigarettes, representing an increase of 4.4 per cent.

A pack of small cigars will go up by 6p and 25g of pipe tobacco by 8p.

Mr Clarke said he was freezing the duty on hand-rolling tobacco this year because it had proved too easy a product to smuggle.

In 1993, Mr Clarke gave a commitment that duty would be raised on tobacco by at least three per cent that year and in future budgets.

"I thought it was the most fair and effective way of backing up health warnings on smoking and I remain convinced of that today," he said.

The British Medical Association said that the increase could save 2,500 lives a year and that the Government should now follow through with other measures, including a ban on tobacco advertising.

Source: The *Telegraph*, November 1995 (following the Budget)

## Data 36D: The relationship between smoking and prices

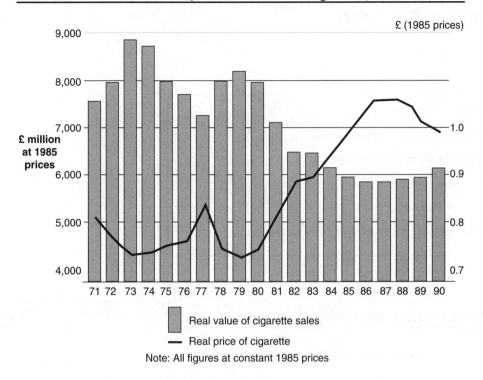

£ (1985 prices)

Real value of cigarette sales

Real price of cigarette

Note: All figures at constant 1985 prices

**Having carefully examined the data in this case study, now answer the following questions.**

## Questions

**a** If the West Midshire is currently providing a combination of 10 'other' operations and 10 heart operations weekly, why could it be said that the hospital is inefficient? Explain how a free market approach might improve the efficiency of the hospital. **(20)**

**b** What 'restrictive practices' might the medical profession currently use to the detriment of patients? **(30)**

**c** Why is smoking considered to be *anti-social* and how could indirect taxation improve the situation? Is there any evidence in the data to suggest that taxes on cigarettes might achieve the desired result? **(20)**

# Money and inflation

This case study contains the following data:

Data 37A    Retail sales and the money supply aggregates

Data 37B    Rise in M0 unlikely to prevent rate cut

Data 37C    High street raises inflation fear

Data 37D    Inflation and money aggregates

Examine all the following data before answering the questions.

## Data 37A: Retail sales and the money supply aggregates

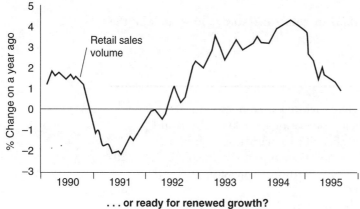

**Is the economy fading fast?**

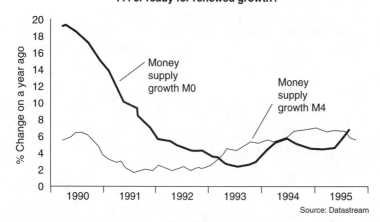

**. . . or ready for renewed growth?**

Source: Datastream

Source: The *Sunday Times*, 1 October 1995

**Data 37B**

# Rise in M0 unlikely to prevent rate cut

## BY ALISDAIR MURRAY

**THE SUPPLY of narrow money, M0, grew unexpectedly strongly last month, although the City regards the rise as insufficient to prevent a quarter-point rate cut, expected on Friday.**

M0 rose 1 per cent in February, according to Bank of England figures published yesterday. On an annual basis, the rise was 6.1 per cent, up from 5.2 per cent in January and well above the 0–4 per cent range set by the Government.

The Treasury described the M0 figures as "erratic", and they are unlikely to be a major point of discussion between Kenneth Clarke, the Chancellor, and the Bank of England when they meet on Thursday.

The Treasury argues that the National Lottery and low of interest rates have meant more people have been holding cash and that a rise in M0 does not necessarily imply a jump in retail sales. Adam Cole, UK economist at James Capel, the broker, said: "Taken at face value, the M0 data clearly point to strong retail sales in February. However, the strength of M0 through most of last year would have been very misleading, given the slowing of retail sales."

The notes and coins element of M0 showed the sharpest rise, to 6.4 per cent in February on an annual basis, from 5.7 per cent in January. Analysts interpreted the growth as signifying some growth in demand this year but said that the CBI distributive trades data to be published on Thursday would give a clearer indication.

Separate data published yesterday showed that Britain's underlying official reserves fell $97 million to $44.95 billion in February.

Source: The *Times*, 4 March 1996

**Data 37C**

# High street raises inflation fear

By Anne Segall, Economics Correspondent

DOUBTS over the wisdom of further interest rate cuts surfaced in the City yesterday after the publication of a Confederation of British Industry survey pointing to strong growth in high street sales in February, a sharp improvement in retail sentiment and higher prices being charged or planned by a broad cross section of retailers.

The CBI distributive trades survey, which is closely monitored by the authorities, suggests that the atmosphere in the high street has been transformed since last summer. Sales are currently rising faster than at any time since August 1993 and retailers are expecting March to be even better than February.

Alistair Eperon, chairman of the CBI's distributive trades survey panel, said: "The rise in volumes for February reported by retailers shows that the momentum in retail trade has extended beyond the Christmas and January sales period." The improving picture also appears to be working its way through the economic chain, with wholesalers claiming that they too had a good February.

The CBI said that the survey findings had taken the urgency out of its recent call for cheaper money as there was clearly no longer a danger of recession. However, it thought a reduction of a ¼ point to 6pc in bank base rates would help underpin consumer confidence.

The monthly monetary meeting between the chancellor, Kenneth Clarke, and Bank of England governor, Eddie George, took place too late yesterday to allow the Bank to make a move in the normal way, through its operations in the money market. A move is, however, expected this morning.

Analysts were nevertheless willing to signal their unease yesterday. Geoffrey Dicks at NatWest Markets said: "Our advice to the chancellor is to be cautious but it is advice that he may not want to hear."

A key cause for concern was evidence that retailers are taking advantage of the more buoyant mood of consumers to push up their prices, with 45pc of firms saying they had raised prices. This could mean that the better inflation picture of recent months could be reversed.

Source: The *Telegraph*, 8 March 1996

## Data 37D: Inflation and money aggregates

The latest inflation report by the Bank of England sees the Bank projecting rates of inflation based on various scenarios. According to the Bank, the rate of inflation could vary anywhere between 4.5% per year to 0.5% per year depending upon the assumptions made.

The Chancellor's decision to cut interest rates in the face of strong monetary growth – whether M0 or M4 – might have benefited by an examination of the Bank's inflation projections. The Bank of England, if not the Chancellor, is certainly concerned about the recent strong growth of the broad money aggregate, M4, which is now growing at almost 10% per year. However, the Bank's report failed to quantify the precise link between the growth of the money supply and the rate of inflation – and perhaps the Chancellor needed that link spelt out.

Bank deposits are certainly piling up in the corporate sector, made flush by the recent burst of mergers and acquisitions. If this cash finds its way into the personal sector by an explosion of bank lending, then look out inflation. Even if the cash finds its way abroad and inflationary pressures are eased this will be at the expense of pressure on sterling.

But it is not only the corporate bank accounts which are buoyant, there is a definite build up in personal bank and building society deposits and this is accelerating the rate of growth of broad money. In itself, odds on, this will lead to a consumer spending spree. In the meantime, however, money is likely to be diverted into other markets such as housing (where there is evidence of this) and the wealth effect stimulated by a healthy housing market will have a multiplier effect on household consumption.

Inflation is back in the equation again.

**Having carefully examined the data in this case study, now answer the following questions.**

## Questions

**a** Distinguish between 'broad money' as measured by M4 and 'narrow money' as measured by M0. Identify the factors which might have contributed to the recent rise in M0. **(30)**

**b** How would the Bank of England 'move in the normal way, through its operations in the money market' to influence interest rates in the short term? **(40)**

**c** Explain how the rate of growth of the money supply – whether M0 or M4 – might be related to the rate of inflation. Why has the government moved over to targeting M0 rather than M4? **(20)**

**d** If the excess money supply finds its way abroad, how might this put pressure on sterling rather than the rate of inflation? **(10)**

# The UK economy

This case study contains the following data:

| | |
|---|---|
| Data 38A | The UK's public sector borrowing requirement 1971–99 (projections) |
| Data 38B | Unemployment in the UK (%) 1971–94 |
| Data 38C | Trade union membership as percentage of civilian workforce in employment, UK, 1971–92 |
| Data 38D | Unemployment rates by region, 1990–94 |
| Data 38E | Employees by industry and gender (Great Britain) (%) |
| Data 38F | Average earnings in Great Britain (1990 = 100) |
| Data 38G | The natural rate of unemployment |

Examine all the following data before answering the questions.

## Data 38A: The UK's public sector borrowing requirement 1971–99 (projections)

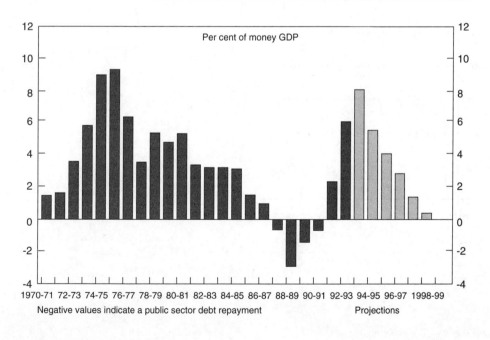

Negative values indicate a public sector debt repayment       Projections

Source: CSO

## Data 38B: Unemployment in the UK (%) 1971–94

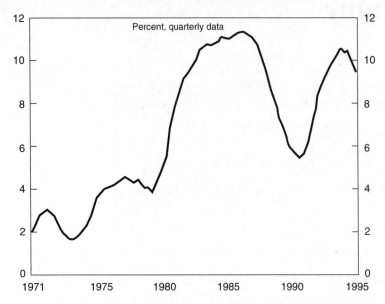

Source: Department of Employment

## Data 38C: Trade union membership as percentage of civilian workforce in employment, UK, 1971–92

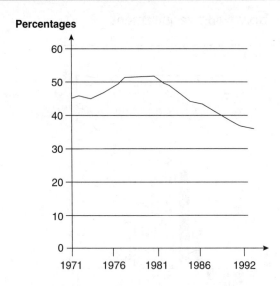

Source: *Social Trends 1995*

## Data 38D: Unemployment rates by region, 1990–94

| | 1990 | 1991 | 1992 | 1993 | 1994 |
|---|---|---|---|---|---|
| | | | | | **Percentages** |
| North | 8.6 | 10.6 | 11.2 | 11.2 | 11.7 |
| Yorkshire and Humberside | 6.8 | 9.1 | 9.9 | 9.8 | 9.8 |
| East Midlands | 5.1 | 7.8 | 8.7 | 9.0 | 8.3 |
| East Anglia | 3.8 | 6.2 | 7.1 | 8.3 | 7.4 |
| South East | 3.9 | 7.4 | 9.4 | 10.3 | 9.6 |
| South West | 4.5 | 7.7 | 9.1 | 9.2 | 7.5 |
| West Midlands | 5.9 | 9.0 | 10.7 | 11.6 | 9.9 |
| North West | 7.5 | 9.9 | 10.1 | 10.9 | 10.2 |
| Wales | 6.6 | 9.2 | 8.9 | 9.5 | 9.4 |
| Scotland | 8.0 | 9.2 | 9.5 | 10.1 | 9.9 |
| Northern Ireland | 13.7 | 14.1 | 12.1 | 12.5 | 11.5 |

Unemployment based on the ILO definition as a percentage of all economically active. At Spring each year

Source: *Social Trends 1995*

## Data 38E:  Employees by industry and gender in Great Britain (%)

| | Males | | | | Females | | | |
|---|---|---|---|---|---|---|---|---|
| | **1971** | **1981** | **1991** | **1994** | **1971** | **1981** | **1991** | **1994** |
| Agriculture | 2 | 2 | 2 | 2 | 1 | 1 | 1 | 1 |
| Energy/water supply | 5 | 5 | 3 | 2 | 1 | 1 | 1 | 1 |
| Manufacturing | 41 | 35 | 29 | 28 | 29 | 19 | 13 | 12 |
| Construction | 8 | 8 | 7 | 6 | 1 | 1 | 1 | 1 |
| Distribution/hotels/ catering/repairs | 13 | 15 | 19 | 20 | 23 | 24 | 25 | 24 |
| Transport/ communication | 10 | 9 | 9 | 9 | 3 | 3 | 3 | 3 |
| Financial/ business services | 5 | 7 | 11 | 13 | 7 | 9 | 13 | 13 |
| Other services | 15 | 18 | 20 | 21 | 35 | 41 | 44 | 45 |
| All employees (100%) = thousands | 13,425 | 12,277 | 11,254 | 10,539 | 8,224 | 9,107 | 10,467 | 10,363 |

Source: *Social Trends 1995*

## Data 38F: Average earnings in Great Britain (1990 = 100)

| Year | Manufacturing industry | Service industries |
|------|------------------------|--------------------|
| **1988** | 84.1 | 83.8 |
| **1989** | 91.4 | 91.2 |
| **1990** | 100.0 | 100.0 |
| **1991** | 108.2 | 107.7 |
| **1992** | 115.3 | 114.1 |
| **1993** | 120.5 | 117.5 |

Source: *Economic Trends 1995* (adapted)

## Data 38G: The natural rate of unemployment

By almost any reckoning a large part of the present level of total unemployment is structural. That means it is beyond the reach of macro-economic policy, and it is unlikely to disappear as a result of the present cyclical expansion. Policies designed towards cutting unemployment can only serve to make matters worse in the short term. The results of trying to reduce unemployment below this 'natural' rate are unstable and potentially explosive for inflation.

The most effective policies to reduce unemployment are those which enhance the flexibility and competitiveness of industry.

(Adapted from a speech by the Governor of the Bank of England, Eddie George, in January 1995)

**Having carefully examined the data in this case study, now answer the following questions.**

## Questions

**a** Examine Data 38B which shows the rate of unemployment in the UK for 1971–94. What correlation (relationships) might you expect between unemployment and each of the following, indicating in your answer whether this correlation can be seen from the data:

   **i** the public sector borrowing requirement (Data 38A)? **(10)**

   **ii** trade union membership (Data 38C)? **(10)**

**b** What evidence is there in the data to support the Governor of the Bank of England's view that structural unemployment is a major problem in the UK economy? **(30)**

**c** Eddie George is an advocate of *supply-side economics*. Explain what he might mean by his comment: 'The most effective policies to reduce unemployment are those which enhance the flexibility and competitiveness of industry.' Give examples of supply-side policies to support your answer. **(30)**

# The economics of alcohol

**This case study contains the following data:**

Data 39A      Shaken but not stirred

Data 39B      Number of breweries in Britain

Data 39C      The price of a pint

Data 39D      Cheap booze is here to stay

Data 39E      Real price of wine before duty, VAT and inflation

Data 39F      Alcohol consumption in the young

Examine all the following data before answering the questions.

## Data 39A: Shaken but not stirred

In 1990, the Monopolies and Mergers Commission undertook a major investigation of the brewing industry and came to the conclusion that the industry was a 'complex monopoly'. The MMC reported that the six biggest brewers in the industry produced 75% of Britain's beer and owned, between them, 75% of 'tied' pubs, ie pubs which are tied to one particular brewery.

As part of its recommendations for the industry, the MMC stated that no one brewer should own more than 5,000 pubs, and that tied tenants should sell at least one 'guest' beer and should be able to buy other drinks from the most competitive suppliers.

## Data 39B: Number of breweries in Britain

| Year | Number of breweries |
|------|---------------------|
| 1900 | 1466 |
| 1910 | 1284 |
| 1920 | 941 |
| 1930 | 559 |
| 1940 | 428 |
| 1950 | 362 |
| 1960 | 247 |
| 1970 | 96 |
| 1980 | 81 |
| 1990 | 65 |
| 1992 | 64 |

Source: Brewer's Society, *Beer Facts 1993*

## Data 39C: The price of a pint

| Year | Price |
|------|-------|
| 1971 | 12p |
| 1974 | 17p |
| 1978 | 23p |
| 1980 | 38p |
| 1984 | 60p |
| 1988 | 68p |
| 1990 | 100p |

Source: The *Guardian*, 13 June 1991

## Data 39D: Cheap booze is here to stay

On 1 January 1993 the Single European Market was introduced with goods flowing freely across European markets, without duty, providing they were purchased by individuals for personal consumption and not for resale. The new rules meant that individuals could go cross-Channel shopping – loading up their cars or vans with cheap French beer or wine and bringing them back into the UK.

Inevitably, the demand for beer in the UK has fallen whilst the demand for French beer has risen. British brewers have claimed that to compensate for falling demand at home the government should reduce the indirect tax levied on beer so that it is much more in line with the French indirect beer tax. The result, on a supply and demand graph, would be to shift the supply of British beer to the right therefore compensating for the lower demand for British beer.

The Treasury has refused on the grounds that the brewers have not got their sums correct. The Treasury proposes that sales of British beer from British pubs has actually increased since 1993 and the impact of the cheap French beer is greater on the take-home market as opposed to the pub market.

## Data 39E: Real price of wine before duty, VAT and inflation (1984 = 100)

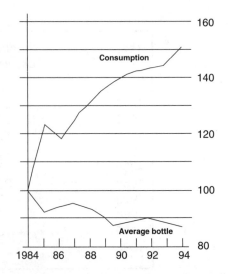

Source: HM Customs & Excise, in Alain Anderton's *The Students' Economy in Focus 1994/95*

122

# Data 39F: Alcohol consumption in the young

In an interview undertaken by the Office of Population Censuses and Surveys, just over one-fifth of children interviewed aged between 11 and 15 years said that their last alcoholic drink had been during the week before they were interviewed. Boys were more likely than girls to have had a drink in the last week.

Three-quarters of those children who said that they had drunk alcohol during the previous week before the interview cited beer, lager or cider as their drinks. The other popular drink was wine – around one in ten children had drunk this in the previous week. The average amount drunk by all drinkers was six units – equivalent to three pints of beer or six glasses of wine.

Alcohol consumption above sensible levels is thought to be associated with increased likelihood of social problems and ill-health. Crime rates, loss of job, loss of self-esteem and moderate to severe ill-health are all related to alcohol consumption.

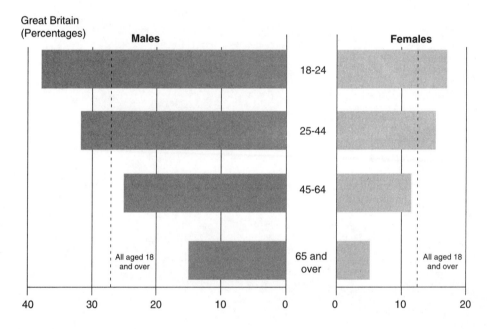

*Note:* sensible levels refer to 21 units per week for men and 14 units per week for women.

Source: *Social Trends 1995*

*Consumption of alcohol above sensible levels: by age and gender, 1992*

**Having carefully examined the data in this case study, now answer the following questions.**

## Questions

**a** What evidence is there, *for* and *against*, the existence of a
monopoly market environment in the brewing industry? **(20)**

**b** Explain, with the aid of a diagram, how the price of wine has
fallen in real terms since 1984. **(20)**

**c** Why does the government place indirect taxes on the
consumption of alcohol? **(40)**

# Manufacturing industry in the UK

This case study contains the following data:

Data 40A     Sterling effective exchange rate (1985 = 100)

Data 40B     UK share of world manufacturing markets

Data 40C     Manufacturing employment, output and productivity

Data 40D     Britain's competitiveness

Data 40E     Bottom of the manufacturing class

Data 40F     Incredible shrinking Britain

Data 40G     The (UK) savings ratio

Examine all the following data before answering the questions.

## Data 40A: Sterling effective exchange rate (1985 = 100)

| Year | 1975 | 1977 | 1979 | 1981 | 1983 | 1985 | 1987 | 1989 | 1991 | 1993 |
|---|---|---|---|---|---|---|---|---|---|---|
| Effective exchange rate | 124.8 | 101.2 | 107.0 | 119.0 | 105.3 | 100.0 | 90.1 | 92.6 | 91.7 | 80.2 |

Source: *Economic Trends 1995*

## Data 40B: UK share of world manufacturing markets

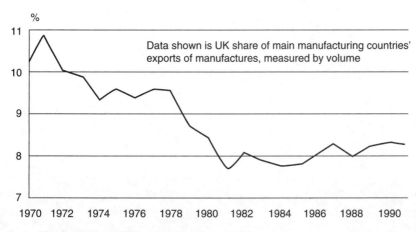

Source: *Lloyds Bank Bulletin,* November 1994

## Data 40C: Manufacturing employment, output and productivity

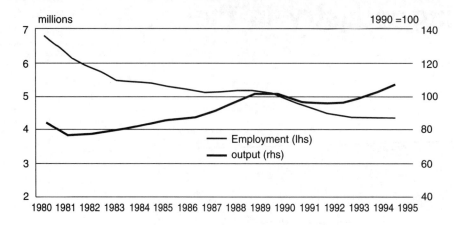

Source: *Lloyds Bank Bulletin*, November 1994

## Data 40D: Britain's competitiveness

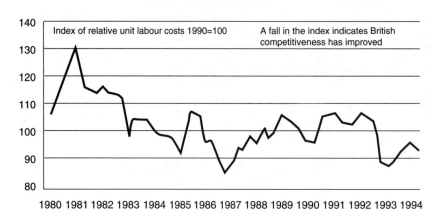

Source: *Lloyds Bank Bulletin*, November 1994

# Data 40E: Bottom of the manufacturing class

**Bottom of the manufacturing class...**

| | Average annual % growth | Total % growth from first to last year | | |
| --- | --- | --- | --- | --- |
| | | 1964-1989 | 1973-1989 | 1973-1992 |
| UK | 1.5 | 41.8 | 8.2 | 1.3 |
| Italy | 3.7 | 138.3 | 39.7 | 68.6 |
| France | 2.9 | 97.2 | 17.5 | 16.5 |
| Germany | 2.7 | 89.4 | 24.0 | 32.1 |
| USA | 3.9 | 150.3 | 58.1 | 55.2 |
| Japan | 6.6 | 963.7 | 69.2 | 68.9 |

**...because we invested too little?**

| | £ million (1990 prices) | Expressed as a % share of manufacturing output |
| --- | --- | --- |
| 1964-1973 | 3614 | 4.0 |
| 1973-1979 | 2146 | 2.1 |
| 1979-1989 | 694 | 0.6 |

**Investment down – unemployment up**

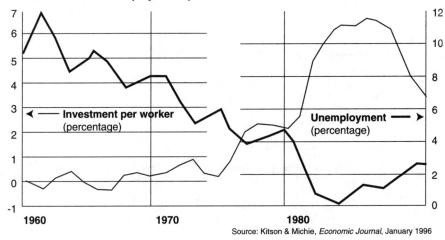

Source: Kitson & Michie, *Economic Journal*, January 1996

Source: The *Observer*, January 1996

# Incredible shrinking Britain

**BOOSTING SAVINGS is just one-half of the medicine to put Britain back on its feet. The other half is the use made of those savings and one of the places it is needed most is Britain's ailing manufacturing industry.**

Research reveals that manufacturing investment in Britain in the 1980s did little more then tread water. New investment was barely sufficient to maintain the 'capital stock' – the manufacturing infrastructure – let alone expand it as our competitor countries have done.

As a result, by the end of the decade German or American workers had, on average, 60% more plant and equipment to work with than British workers. Research shows that investment by manufacturing firms had plummeted to a mere £694 million between 1979 and 1989.

However hard the remaining employees worked they could not compensate for the dramatic shrinking of the UK's industrial base. This is a very different picture from the one painted by the government, with its repeated claims that productivity rose during the 1980s. Output per worker did increase, but primarily because there were fewer workers rather than because Britain was producing more goods.

Three million jobs in manufacturing have been lost in Britain since 1979 – a much bigger drop than in any other industrialised country. At the macro level this decline in manufacturing has had a number of worrying consequences. In particular, the resultant rise in the trade deficit had led to volatile interest rates which have their damaging effect on investment levels and business confidence. This was very apparent in the early 1980s when high interest rates caused cash flow problems for many companies and led to bankruptcies and closures. They also contributed to the over-valuation of sterling, which in turn priced UK goods out of world markets.

If the damaging decline in manufacturing is to be reversed, the starting point must be higher investment levels. However, these will not be achieved by boosting company profits. Profits went up in the 1980s, but instead of fuelling investment, they were used to raise dividends to shareholders.

(Adapted from an article by Michael Kitson and Jonathan Michie, The *Observer*, January 1996)

## Data 40G: The UK savings ratio (figures rounded)

| Year | Savings ratio (savings as a % of personal disposable income) |
|------|------|
| 1983 | 9.7 |
| 1984 | 11.1 |
| 1985 | 10.7 |
| 1986 | 8.7 |
| 1987 | 7.1 |
| 1988 | 5.7 |
| 1989 | 7.2 |
| 1990 | 8.4 |
| 1991 | 10.5 |
| 1992 | 12.8 |
| 1993 | 12.2 |

Source: *Economic Trends 1995*

**Having carefully examined the data in this case study, now answer the following questions.**

## Questions

a  Describe and explain the trend in manufacturing *productivity* between 1980 and 1994. **(10)**

b  Describe the trend in the UK's share of manufacturing markets between 1970 and 1995. Give reasons to account for this trend. **(70)**

# Answers

## Case Study 36: A step forward for health care?

**a**  A combination of 10 heart operations and 10 'other' operations can be regarded as being both allocative and productive inefficient. Such a combination lies within the production possibility curve for the West Midshire and therefore either some resources are not being used at all or the existing resources are not being used to their full potential. In either case, a move towards a combination of operations on the production possibility curve represents an improvement in both allocative and productive efficiency.

A free market approach to hospital services will improve the efficiency of the hospital in several ways. First, a free market must respond to consumer demands and in the case of the West Midshire that means providing the services which consumers – the patients – demand the most. This will improve allocative efficiency. In a truly competitive market the final price of a good or service will be equal to the marginal production costs indicating that consumers want no more and no less of a certain service/product. This implies perfect resource allocation.

A free market also improves productive efficiency as the hospital becomes much more cost-conscious. In this respect, the provision of patient services and care becomes much more akin to the minimum average costs of production.

**b**  'Restrictive practices' in the provision of health care refers to any practice which limits the supply of operations and other medical services to the benefit of the practitioner's pocket rather than to the benefit of the patient. For instance, restrictive practices could refer to a limit on the number of operations scheduled during the working day. If the practitioners agree, collectively, to restrict their operating lists or ward rounds then, obviously, there is more likelihood of those surgeons earning higher earnings from the NHS. A further development of this is the possibility of the surgeons suggesting to patients that to avoid long delays on the NHS, private consultations are necessary.

Surgeons work in 'firms' and each firm is recognised for a certain specialism. If the 'firms' informally agree only to provide a narrow range of specialisms and to refer other cases to other firms, then there is a possibility that this will work to the disadvantage of the patient who may have to wait longer for treatment. Competition in all its forms can only benefit the patient.

**c**  Smoking imposes an adverse externality on the community in the form of the effects of passive smoking and the added burden on the services of the NHS. Without government interference, the market mechanisms would result in a cigarette price where the marginal private costs (the supply curve) would just be equal to the marginal benefit to consumers (the demand curve). This is illustrated in the diagram below and gives rise to a price of $P_1$ when $Q_1$ packets are purchased.

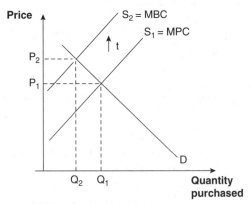

MBC = Marginal benefit to consumers
MPC = Marginal private cost

However, the full social costs of smoking are much higher than the private costs due to the adverse externalities caused by smokers. The market price needs to be pushed up to $P_2$ so that the marginal benefit curve is equal to the marginal social cost curve. This can be achieved by levying an indirect tax, of t, onto the cigarettes. Notice that by so doing the demand for cigarettes will fall, causing the adverse externalities to be diminished. Naturally, the success of the tax in stopping consumers smoking will depend crucially upon the price elasticity of demand for the cigarettes.

Of course, the tax revenue raised by the government can be used partially to provide for the services of the NHS and this, too, helps to internalise the adverse externality.

There is some evidence in the data to suggest that higher prices, accompanied by health warnings, will be successful. The British Medical Association reports that an increase of 15p on a packet of 20 cigarettes will save 2,500 lives in one year. Further, **Data 36D** suggests that there is a clear indirect relationship between cigarette sales and the price of cigarettes in real terms. As cigarette prices fall in real terms, so sales increase and vice versa.

# Answers

## Case Study 37: Money and inflation

**a** In the UK we have two official monetary aggregates – M0 and M4 – for which the Treasury set monitoring ranges. These are currently: M0 = 0–4%; and M4 = 3–9%.

Although the Treasury set a range for both aggregates it is only for M0 that a actual target objective is set.

M0 is often described as 'narrow' money and it is a measure of the notes and coins in circulation plus banker's voluntary deposits at the Bank of England. The government has set a target range of 0–4% growth in M0 per annum. It is currently running at some 6.1%.

M4 is often described as 'broad' money and it is a measure of M0 plus all current and deposit accounts held by the private sector in sterling at banks and building societies. M4 also includes the holding of sterling certificates of deposit by the private sector. M4 is an indication of future spending power in the longer term rather than the short term and is also a measure of the lending activities of the banking sector. The target range for M4 is 3–9% growth rate per year. Currently, M4 is growing at 9.9% per annum.

The recent rise in M0 could be the result of several factors. First, there is evidence provided by the CBI that retail sales are increasing and this will reflect very closely and very quickly in a surge of M0. The CBI stresses that there was a strong growth in retail sales in February and, following this, there is pressure on prices to rise. Retailers in the High Street appear to want to take advantage of the increased consumer demand by pushing up their prices in the months ahead.

Secondly, there is a suggestion that the National Lottery has had an impact on M0 as millions of individuals chance their luck with their Lottery tickets.

Thirdly, the low rates of interest currently available in savings and deposit accounts increase the attractiveness of cash assets rather than illiquid assets.

There are further considerations which have not been taken into account by the data. As the growth of part-time employment continues, the growth of M0 can be expected since part-timers are more likely to be paid in cash than full-timers. Another factor is the size of the black economy. For tax reasons, those participating in the black economy prefer to be paid in cash rather than put their takings through bank accounts.

**b** The Bank of England controls short-term interest rates by working through the 'money market'. If the Bank of England, on behalf of the government, wishes to increase interest rates in the economy then the Bank will need to starve the financial system of liquidity before lending the banks the money they need at a rate of interest which the Bank decides. This rate of interest – the rate which the Bank of England charges when financial institutions are forced to borrow as 'a last resort' – is called the *bank rate* or the *minimum lending rate*.

The Bank of England operates in the money market on a daily basis to influence short-term interest rates. Transactions between the commercial banks are settled by transfers between accounts which are centrally held at the Bank of England. The banks are expected to have a positive balance on their account at the Bank of England on a daily basis. Transactions between the banks do not alter the total amount of funds on their accounts at the Bank of England; they merely redistribute funds between them. But transactions between the Bank of England and the banking system do affect the total. For example, if the Bank of England issues its notes to the commercial banks, these are paid for by running down the banks' accounts at the Bank. Since the government also keeps its main accounts at the Bank of England, transactions between the government and the private sector also affect the total balances held by the commercial banks at the Bank. Payments from the privates sector to the government are finally settled by a transfer of funds between the commercial banks' accounts at the Bank and one of the government's accounts.

If on a particular day there is a net flow of funds from the private sector to the government's accounts – perhaps tax bills are being paid or individuals are buying government stock – then the banking system will find it difficult to maintain a positive balance on its accounts at the Bank of England. Normally, the commercial banks start each day anticipating that they will face a shortage of funds and the Bank of England will aim to relieve that prospective shortage by buying commercial bills off financial institutions in the money market. As the bills are purchased by the Bank of England, so funds are transferred back into the commercial banks' accounts and the shortage is relieved. It is by setting the interest rates on these operations that the Bank of England influences the general level of interest rates across the economy.

The Bank's daily operations to relieve the shortage are conducted mainly through a small group of intermediaries called *discount houses*. They are invited to offer for sale, to the Bank, bills which they own or which they can acquire from the banks. Depending on the size of the expected shortage, up to three rounds of operations may be held each day. If these operations are not sufficient to relieve the shortage, the Bank of England will be prepared to lend to the discount houses charging the minimum lending rate or bank rate.

Interest rates in the money market will generally be close to those at which the Bank conducts its operations. If the Chancellor decides that a change in short-term interest rates is appropriate, the Bank will signal this by changing the level of rates at which it is prepared to relive the shortage. Any such change will normally be reflected quickly in money market rates in general and in bank base rates, i.e. the rates they use to calculate their customer rates. The Bank may also signal its intentions by announcing in advance the rate at which it will lend to the discount houses. This official announcement is only made in extenuating circumstances.

c The data suggests that the Chancellor might have benefited from the Bank of England being more specific about how the rate of growth of the money supply – whether M0 or M4 – might be related to the rate of inflation. According to monetarists, rises in the rate of growth of the money supply are likely to lead to price inflation. An increase in M0 or M4 signals that purchasing power in the economy is rising aided by bank lending and credit creation. As demand builds up, and without appropriate increases in the supply of goods and services, so pressure in the economy leads to rising price levels and inflation sets in. The Bank of England's inflation report is suggesting that future inflation could be anywhere between 4.5% per annum and 0.5% per annum depending on various scenarios such as productivity gains, interest rates and rate of growth of the money supply.

M0 is a measure of immediate purchasing power and this is where its strength lies. A recorded increase in M0 will tend to imply that inflation will rise in the near future as the economy increases its expenditure levels. M4 was dropped as an intermediate target objective mainly because the expected predictable relationship between growth of M4 and aggregate demand/national income did not materialise in the 1980s.

Liberalisation of the banking system led to an increase in the velocity of money in circulation which tended to rule out the effect of money growth restraint on levels of aggregate demand. The government therefore moved over to intermediate targeting of M0 rather than the erratic M4. Data for M0 is available weekly and therefore it is a good short-term indicator. Also since cash tends to be held by individuals rather than companies, M0 gives a good indication of current behaviour of consumer expenditure and retail sales, and ultimately inflation rates.

d If the excess money supply finds its way abroad in the form of increased expenditure on imports then it is possible that inflation will slow. However, as the demand for imports

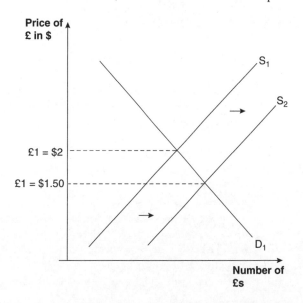

from abroad rises so the value of sterling is likely to fall as is illustrated above.

The value of sterling is originally given by £1 = $2, where the demand for sterling is equal to the supply of sterling on the foreign exchange market. If the demand for imports rise, then in order to pay for the extra imports more sterling will enter the foreign exchange market to be changed into foreign currencies in order to pay for the imports. Thus the supply of sterling increases from $S_1$ to $S_2$. All other things being constant the value of sterling will now fall to a lower level where the demand for sterling is now equal to the new supply of sterling as given by $S_2$. The new equilibrium will therefore be £1 = $1.50.

# Answers

## Case Study 38: The UK economy

a  i  **Unemployment and the PSBR**: The PSBR measures the difference between the expenditure and income of the public sector. If public spending exceeds the revenue from taxes and other sources, e.g. privatisation proceeds, then the government must become a net borrower giving rise to a PSBR. The size of the PSBR has given rise to a lot of attention in the 1990s as it reached a peak of almost £50 billion during 1994. One would expect a close correlation between the size of the PSBR and the measured level of unemployment. As unemployment rises so revenue from direct income taxes and, indeed, indirect expenditure taxes will diminish. At the same time, the government will be forced to spend more on welfare payments such as unemployment benefit thus giving rise to a growing PSBR.

The data given provides some evidence of this relationship – although not perfect evidence. From 1971 to 1985 there is a long-term trend of rising unemployment (interrupted by some periods of slightly falling levels of unemployment). The PSBR in this period was always positive, but the correlation is not perfect. For instance, in 1974 unemployment was at its lowest for the whole of the period, but the PSBR was a significant 6% of GDP. Similarly, the PSBR reaches a peak in 1976 whilst unemployment for that year was a fairly modest 4% of the labour force. Certainly time lags might be important in this correlation. In 1986 unemployment reaches a peak of some 11% whilst the PSBR was a modest 1% of GDP. Clearly, there must be other sources of government revenue to cope with the rising tide of unemployment – privatisation proceeds!

The correlation between unemployment and the PSBR is much closer in the latter period. The noticeable slump in unemployment from 1986 to 1990 coincides with the PSBR moving into a period of PSDR (public sector debt repayment). The government is paying back debts of the past. The correlation continues into the early 1990s with rising unemployment and rising PSBRs.

ii  **Unemployment and trade union membership:** One would expect trade union membership and unemployment to be inversely related. As unemployment rises so the trade union membership can be expected to fall. As unemployment increases those made unemployed see relatively little point in remaining trade union members, even at reduced rate subscriptions. In addition, the fear of growing unemployment seems to be a natural check on the strength of trade unions and individual workers might regard trade unions as a relatively expensive and ineffective accessory to work.

Once again the evidence proves inconclusive. Between 1971 and 1980 the level of unemployment and trade union membership rose and fell directly with each other rather than inversely. Presumably the growth of unemployment from a low base line did not counteract the perceived power of the trade unions in achieving high pay awards. Workers were prepared to risk unemployment if their unions were able to secure high wage increases, even if real wages were falling at the time due to accelerating inflation. From 1980 until 1986 there was a very significant rise in unemployment. Many would attribute this to the onset of monetary economics which sought to control the rate of growth of the money supply so as to restrain inflation. During this period, trade union membership fell very significantly. Certainly, the rapid growth in unemployment was a very significant factor in reducing union membership. In addition, however, mention must be made of the trade union restrictions imposed by the government during this period which, although improving flexibility in the labour market, had the effect of reducing the power of the trade union movement: that movement has never since recovered. From 1986 to 1990 unemployment levels fell as the economy made a recovery, but union membership continued to fall.

Clearly, there are other factors in determining trade union membership. Union image has become somewhat outdated and the new generation of workers have to be wooed back into the movement. Also there are significant changes in the labour market which contribute to the decline in union membership which continues. Full-time jobs in manufacturing – a traditionally male dominated sector – are disappearing, to be replaced with part-time jobs in the service sector – a traditionally female dominated sector. The moves from full-time to part-time, male to female, manufacturing to service, all have a negative impact on trade union membership.

**b** Structural unemployment refers to long-term unemployment where there is a permanent mismatch between the demand for labour and the supply of labour. On a regional basis, certain areas of the country suffer from structural unemployment. Many regions have specialised in certain products, often because of natural resources, and built up their employment opportunities based on the one industry. When that industry suffers decline due to falling demand, the region is characterised by heavy unemployment and few new job opportunities. In a perfect world the labour made available in these regions should transfer to other regions of the country where there is a demand for extra workers. But labour immobility, both geographical and occupational, results in permanent high levels of unemployment in certain regions of the UK.

The data suggests that structural unemployment of this nature is occurring in Northern Ireland, the West Midlands, the North and the North West where unemployment rates seem consistently higher than in other areas.

Structural unemployment is also associated with the loss of markets caused by increased competition from abroad. The tremendous competition from the less developed countries of the Pacific Rim and elsewhere has had a very negative impact on jobs in manufacturing industry in the UK. The evidence from the data supports rising structural unemployment as our traditional manufacturing jobs disappear. **Data 38E** reveals severe job losses for males and females in manufacturing with little gain for the males elsewhere, apart from the service sector. Female employment tends to be holding its own with new jobs being created in the service sector in particular.

Advances in technology tend to contribute to structural unemployment. Groups of workers across industries may be put out of work by new technology, and without retraining and geographical mobility these workers may remain unemployed for long periods of time.

Some economists would argue that structural unemployment would fall if workers were prepared to accept lower wages – a wage which would equate the demand for labour with the supply of labour. There is evidence in the data, however, to suggest wage rigidity especially in manufacturing industry. Given that over the period, manufacturing jobs have disappeared significantly (whilst service sector jobs have grown), one would expect depressed wage rates in the manufacturing sector compared to the service sector. **Data 38F** provides evidence that this is not so. Average earnings in both sectors are very similar which tends to give credence to the idea that the UK economy is characterised by a 'wage differential' philosophy. We cling to a traditional wage level ladder regardless of demand and supply of labour conditions.

**c** Supply-side economics refers to economic policies which work on the aggregate supply side of the economy rather than the aggregate demand side. Consider the following diagram:

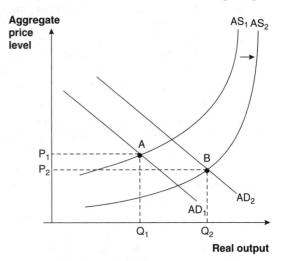

AS = Agregate supply
AD = Aggregate demand

Initially, the macro-economic equilibrium is at A, with a price level of $P_1$ and aggregate output of $Q_1$. Demand stimulating policies will cause the aggregate demand curve to shift to the right which brings about more output and hence more jobs but at the expense of higher price levels. If the government prefers to stimulate the economy by supply-side measures, the aggregate supply curve will shift to the right which results in a new equilibrium at B which corresponds to higher levels of output (and hence more jobs) with a lower price level.

Supply-side policies are usually centred on the following:

- *Tax reforms* which involve reducing the marginal rate of taxation for both individuals and companies. The former creates more of an incentive to work and thus improves the flexibility and competitiveness of the labour market; whilst the latter allows companies to retain more of their profits which can be ploughed back into the companies.
- *Labour market reforms* which are aimed at creating a more flexible labour market which is eager to work at existing wage levels and is less encumbered by the impediments created by trade unions. Further labour market reforms usually concentrate on improving the skills and the willingness of the labour force to adapt to new working arrangements such as part-time and job sharing arrangements.
- *Privatisation* of once state-owned industries to create a more competitive environment for industry and to encourage a wider and deeper share ownership which can eventually result in long-lasting sources of finance for industry.
- *Deregulation* of the market to remove barriers, bureaucracy and red tape which stifles real competition and creates an unhealthy, lethargic industry.

# Answers

## Case Study 39: The economics of alcohol

**a** The text book definition of a *monopolist* is that it is a sole producer of a good for which there are few substitutes. On the basis of this definition there is little evidence for a monopoly in the brewing industry: there are six large breweries in operation in the UK, plus a number of smaller breweries. In addition, the data is suggesting that there are close substitutes in the form of wine and cider and, further, the introduction of the Single Market has resulted in close substitutes being available on the Continent at competitive prices. This has been aided by the opening of the Eurotunnel which has reduced Channel crossing times.

However, the working definition of a *monopolist* is that it is a company which has at least 25% of the market and there is plenty of evidence that using this definition there is some degree of monopoly status in the UK brewing industry. For one thing, the Monopolies and Mergers Commission would not investigate the industry unless it felt that an existing monopoly was in practice or that a future merger might result in a potential monopoly which might act 'against the public interest'. The final report by the MMC gave evidence that the biggest breweries were controlling very large slices of the pub trade and by operating on a tied basis were reducing the choice for consumers and the possibility of new entrants from breaking into the market. Further evidence is found by an examination of the number of breweries in Britain (**Data 39B**).

There has been a very significant decrease in independent brewers as, in turn, they get bought up and forced out of business by the very big brewers. As competition is reduced so the price of a pint of beer has increased in real terms – another feature of monopoly markets. Beer prices have been consistently rising over the period. The brewers would point to rising production costs as being the source of the continuous price hike. However, there is sufficient evidence in the data to suggest that the imperfect market (to say the least) in the brewing industry is responsible for eliminating competition in the alcoholic drinks trade.

**b** The price of wine has fallen in real terms since 1984 and the data suggests that consumption of wine has correspondingly increased. In economic terms there has been a movement along the demand curve for wine. However there is more to the wine market than is illustrated in the following diagram:

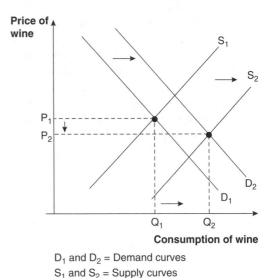

$D_1$ and $D_2$ = Demand curves
$S_1$ and $S_2$ = Supply curves

*The wine market*

The price of beer, a substitute for wine, has consistently risen over the period and the effect of this is to cause the demand for wine to shift to the right – a shift which is enhanced by the growing popularity and fashion of wine drinking. Therefore the demand for wine has shifted from $D_1$ to $D_2$. All things being equal, a shift to the right of the demand curve will cause the price of the good or service to rise. The apparent failure of the price of wine to rise despite an increase in its demand must be viewed against the backdrop of substantial increases in the supply of wine onto UK markets. Not only is it increasingly convenient and cheaper to cross the Channel in search of wine, but also many new countries are moving into the wine market – notice the Australian, Bulgarian and Chilean wines on the supermarket shelf. Therefore the supply of wine has shifted from $S_1$ to $S_2$. Given $S_2$ and $D_2$, the new equilibrium price of wine is $P_2$ (compared to $P_1$) and $Q_2$ bottles of wine are now purchased, instead of $Q_1$.

The fall in the price of wine has certainly been aided by economies of scale in purchasing made possible by large retail outlets such as

# Answers

hypermarkets and off licences. Large buying power from these organisations can force wine producers to reduce their profit margins in return for large contracts to buy from hypermarkets and off licences. These can then pass the savings partially on to the consumer in the form of lower retail prices.

c There is plenty of evidence that alcohol abuse imposes adverse externalities on the community. The data provided indicates that drinking amongst the young is on the increase and that consumption of alcohol above sensible levels in more prevalent in the younger age range. The problems associated with alcohol abuse are increasing crime rates, ill health and an inability to hold a job down. Economists will view alcohol abuse somewhat differently from the sociologist. The inability to hold down a job will first have repercussions on the aggregate supply curve which is partially dependent upon a well-trained, motivated and flexible workforce. It is desirable for aggregate supply curves to shift rightwards over time, resulting in higher levels of output at lower prices.

There is also a severe opportunity cost involved. If alcohol abuse means that individuals are unable to maintain their jobs, then not only does the economy lose out on their output, but the unemployment benefit which the individual is now entitled to could have been used elsewhere in the economy – on education or the National Health Service perhaps. Similarly, the loss of tax revenue is another opportunity cost.

Further problems arise because alcohol abuse requires medical care and the NHS will need to budget for such needs. Again there is an opportunity cost in the sense that other medical services might have to be cut to cater for alcohol related medical care. Finally, drunk individuals are costly to police and often demonstrate a disregard for the property of others.

The government needs to find some way of reducing the extent of alcohol abuse and this is undertaken by indirect taxation. Consider the diagram below.

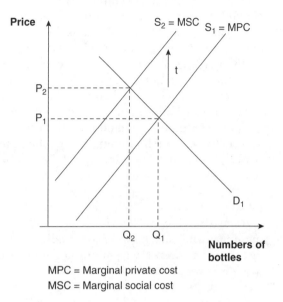

MPC = Marginal private cost
MSC = Marginal social cost

*The whisky market*

Without government intervention the price of a bottle of whisky would settle at $P_1$ with $Q_1$ bottles being consumed. This is where the demand for whisky is equal to the marginal private costs of production – the supply curve for whisky. However, whisky consumption can involve some adverse externalities as explained earlier and as reflected in the marginal social costs curve rather than the marginal private cost curve. The socially efficient production of wine should therefore be $Q_2$ at a market price of $P_2$. In order to achieve this more desirable consumption level, the government imposes an indirect tax of t onto whisky producers.

Notice that not only will fewer bottles be sold and drunk, but that the tax revenue so earned from the tax on whisky can be used positively to reduce the effects of alcohol abuse on the community.

### Case Study 40: Manufacturing industry in the UK

a   Between 1980 and 1990 manufacturing output consistently increased even though the number of employees involved in manufacturing consistently decreased. Therefore it must be inferred that output per person-productivity consistently increased in this period. From 1990 to 1992 there was a fall in manufacturing output, followed by an continued increase in output. Again, in this period, employment opportunities have continued to fall (although there does appear to be some bottoming out in the latter period). One must assume, again, that output per person has increased in manufacturing.

b   Between 1970 and 1990 there has been a marked decrease in the UK's share of world manufacturing markets. Traditionally, manufacturing has been a very important source of foreign revenue to the UK economy and that source is noticeably diminishing. This is reflected in the comparison of average annual growth rates in manufacturing (**Data 40E**) which indicates that manufacturing growth in the UK is the lowest (1.5%) out of six selected countries. What has happened to our manufacturing industry?

   The data suggests that one of our problems is lack of investment in new technology and equipment. It is suggested that there is an inverse relationship between new investment and the level of unemployment, particularly in manufacturing industry. In the 1980s, UK manufacturing infrastructure barely 'trod water' whilst foreign competitors were expanding their investment levels. German and American workers had 60% more plant and equipment by the end of the decade compared to their UK counterparts. Simple Keynesian economics will tell us that investment is one of the three injections into the circular flow of income and that a rise in any of these injections will have positive repercussions on the level of national income expenditure and output – dependent upon the size of the injections multiplier. Keynesian economics also tells us that investment is a particularly volatile injection depending to a large degree on expectations about the state of the economy and the future. How can more investment in manufacturing help us to recapture our lost markets?

   New investment allows a company to increase its productive capacity and ultimately this will allow the supply curve to shift to the right, which then allows the price of the product to fall to more competitive levels. We need to compete on a price basis with the products from many of the less-developed countries. At the moment we out-price ourselves from the world markets. Investment also allows a company to improve the quality of the product or to move into new product areas which, again, is very important in recapturing markets. Finally, investment in new technology will improve delivery dates for new orders.

   One might question why investment levels seem to be so low compared to our competitors. The data suggests that one major factor is a lack of personal savings which provides the finance, through financial intermediaries, for companies to fund their investment levels. The data suggests that in the 1980s the savings ratio, which measures the proportion of our income we save, behaved in a roller coaster fashion. Private industry needs a stable savings ratio with preferably low interest rates. Interest rates reached 15% in 1990, but have subsequently been reduced following the UK's departure from the ERM in 1992 and the government's efforts to revive the economy since then. In order to maintain such high interest rates in the economy in the latter part of the 1980s and early 1990s the government was forced to maintain a very high level of public sector borrowing (PSBR) which, in turn, had repercussions for crowding out private investment.

   Another area which has caused concern and contributed to lost markets is the UK's so-called 'skills gap'. Evidence suggests that manufacturing industry in the UK is suffering from a deficiency in certain skills and lack of vocational training of the workforce. The UK needs more human investment as well as investment in technology. More flexibility and appropriate skills in the labour force will allow UK companies to compete more effectively with foreign manufacturers. Another factor which is important, as regards the labour force and loss of manufacturing markets, concerns the cost of labour. If wage rates are seriously above those of our competitors then this will, in turn, affect the price of the product on the world market. The data is suggesting that UK wage costs have been erratic over the period 1980–94, but that there is an overall tendency for real wage rates to fall.

In theory, the value of a currency on international markets should have an influence in determining the success of a country in obtaining foreign markets. If the value of the currency is low, then imports become relatively expensive and exports relatively cheap. This causes a fall in the demand for imports and a rise in the demand for exports – assuming the demand for imports and exports is sufficiently price elastic. Throughout the period 1975–94, the effective exchange rate for sterling fell consistently, but the loss of manufacturing markets continued. Presumably the demand for manufacturing imports and exports is insufficiently price elastic. The UK has been running a current account deficit on the overall balance of payments consistently since 1986 (although the current account with other EU countries is, in fact, in surplus).

The government's forecasts for the overall current account predict that it will remain a deficit for the foreseeable future. In such a situation, the deficit has to be paid for by borrowing, but some economists believe that by the year 2000 accumulated interest repayments on our external borrowing could run to £10–£15 billion. Eventually, lenders to the UK will come to see that the UK is a bad risk and no further funds will be made available. At such time the economy can be expected to move into a severe recession with the value of sterling plummeting. This might revive the export market in manufacturing and the volume of imports might be choked off by demand-reducing polices such as higher personal income tax and high rates of interest. All things being equal, economic growth could become negative.

# TOPIC INFORMATION TABLES

The following tables provide information for teachers and students on the topic contents of each set of questions. This should assist teachers in integrating the use of the questions with their scheme of work.

## Section A

| Data title | | Topic |
|---|---|---|
| **1** | Rightway Electronics | * Short term versus long term<br>* Law of diminishing returns<br>* Economies and diseconomies of scale |
| **2** | West Midshire Trust Hospital | * Concept of merit goods<br>* Demand and supply analysis<br>* Opportunity cost |
| **3** | Assembly Techniques Limited | * Profit calculation<br>* Price elasticity of demand<br>* Responding to a change in fixed costs |
| **4** | Production possibilities | * Concept of production possibility curves<br>* Economic growth |
| **5** | Star Enterprise | * Profit maximisation concept<br>* Total revenue maximisation<br>* Allocative efficiency |
| **6** | EU farm burden slated | * Minimum prices-agriculture<br>* Demand and supply analysis |
| **7** | ICI's grand acquisitors | * Internal growth<br>* Types of takeovers/mergers<br>* Economies and diseconomies of scale |
| **8** | The end of a chapter | * Fixed price agreements<br>* Price elasticity and revenue<br>* Price wars |
| **9** | Oil price fall world wide | * Costs of production<br>* Cartels<br>* Demand and supply analysis |
| **10** | Level house prices likely | * Demand and supply analysis<br>* Interest rates |

# Section B

| Data title | Topic |
|------------|-------|
| **11** The route to EMU | * Budget deficits <br> * The single currency <br> * The effect of changes of interest on the economy |
| **12** Welsh paying through the nose for petrol | * Free market mechanism <br> * Cartels <br> * Oligopoly |
| **13** Developing countries | * Growing importance of LDCs <br> * Measured GDP and standards of living <br> * Command to market economies |
| **14** An integrated transport system | * Privatisation <br> * Activities of the MMC <br> * Production costs <br> * Price elasticity of demand and profit/revenue |
| **15** Rate rise hangs on pound | * Effect of interest rates on sterling <br> * Relationship between interest rates and inflation <br> * Measuring inflation |
| **16** Rise of the superpower | * Functions of the MMC <br> * Privatisation <br> * Competition, choice and efficiency |
| **17** Potatoes boil as famine fears fuel futures | * Price instability <br> * Demand and supply analysis <br> * Cross elasticity of demand |
| **18** Diamond deal heralds a retreat from the abyss | * Cartels <br> * Factors influencing break-up of cartel <br> * Price and marginal utility |
| **19** Balnce of payments accounting | * Measurement of current account and interpretation of trends <br> * Policies to correct deficits |
| **20** The UK's balance of trade regarding countries outside the EU | * Trade deficits <br> * Devaluation of currency <br> * Investment, multiplier and national income <br> * Economic recovery and growth |
| **21** The savings ratio | * Personal disposable income <br> * Factors influencing savings <br> * Effects of changes in savings ratios on economy |

**Section B continued**

| Data title | Topic |
|---|---|
| 22  Measuring inflation | * Calculation of RPI<br>* Interpretation of RPI against individual's standards of living |
| 23  Tories plan U-turn on car culture | * Adverse externalities<br>* Policies to cope with adverse externalities<br>* Price elasticity of demand |
| 24  Minister condemns EU over tobacco farm aid | * Adverse externalities<br>* Imperfect allocation of resources<br>* EU farm policy |
| 25  Government finances | * Economic growth constraints<br>* Effect of interest rate changes<br>* PSBR<br>* Balanced budgets |

# Section C

| Data title | Topic |
|---|---|
| ∨ 26  The M&S of water – a step ahead of demand | * Characteristics of monopoly<br>* Adverse externalities<br>* Efficiency and privatisation<br>* Profit and shareholders |
| 27  The effective exchange rate | * Effective exchange rate versus single currency<br>* Exchange rates and balance of payments<br>* Causes of changes in exchange rates |
| 28  The Utopian economy | * Consumption functions<br>* Equilibrium national income<br>* Multiplier concept<br>* Budgetary changes |
| 29  Bankers declare war on currency dealers | * Floating exchange rates theory<br>* Central banks and exchange rates<br>* Causes of changes in currency values |
| 30  Dairy farmers go down the drain | * EU farm policy<br>* Deregulation of UK milk industry<br>* Quotas |
| 31  Don't shoot the economist | * Theory of perfect competition<br>* Resource and productive efficiency in a perfect market<br>* Price elasticity of demand<br>* Relevant economic theory |

| Data title | Topic |
|---|---|
| **32** Freedom to work is not a part-time principle | * Deregulation and flexibility in the labour market<br>* Interest rates and value of currency<br>* Keynesian demand management policies<br>* Part-time employment growth and effects |
| **33** Minimum wages spell maximum harm | * Minimum wage legislation<br>* Wage differentials<br>* Cost–push inflation<br>* Effects of high interest rates on economy |
| **34** A recovery faltering through lack of investment | * Effects of devaluation on competitiveness<br>* Supply-side economic policies<br>* Importance of investment in economy<br>* Government influence on private investment |
| **35** Unemployment | * Cyclical versus structural unemployment<br>* Natural level of unemployment<br>* Phillips curves – short- and long-term<br>* Changes in natural level of unemployment over time |

# Section D

| Case study | Topic |
|---|---|
| **36** A step forward for health care? | * Production possibility frontiers<br>* Monopolies – restrictive practices<br>* Private costs versus social costs<br>* Indirect taxation |
| **37** Money and inflation | * Money supply aggregates<br>* Bank of England and the money market<br>* Money supply aggregates and inflation<br>* Floating exchange rates |
| **38** The UK economy | * Unemployment and the PSBR<br>* Unemployment and trade union membership<br>* Types of unemployment<br>* Supply-side economic policies |

## Section D continued

| Data title | Topic |
|---|---|
| **39**   The economics of alcohol | *   Monopoly markets<br>*   Demand and supply analysis<br>*   Indirect taxation |
| **40**   Manufacturing industry in the UK | *   Trends in manufacturing productivity<br>*   International comparisons in manufacturing productivity<br>*   Importance of investment<br>*   Savings ratios |